HIGH JUMP

Frank W. Dick O.B.E.

(*B.A.F. Director of Coaching*)

First published   1949 (G. H. G. Dyson)
Second Edition   1951 (D. C. V. Watts)
Third Edition   1953 (D. C. V. Watts)
Fourth Edition   1957 (D. C. V. Watts)
Fifth Edition   1964 (D. C. V. Watts)
Sixth Edition   1969 (D. C. V. Watts)
Seventh Edition   1975 (Frank W. Dick)
Eighth Edition   1980 (Frank W. Dick)
This Edition   1993 (Frank W. Dick)

ISBN 0 85134 112 8   3M/49M/7.93

©BRITISH ATHLETIC FEDERATION
225A Bristol Road,
Birmingham B5 7UB

Typeset in Times by BPCC Whitefriars,
printed on 115 gsm Fineblade Cartridge and
bound in England by BPCC Wheatons.

About the Author

FRANK W. DICK, O.B.E., F.B.I.S.C., B.Sc, D.L.C.
Frank Dick is a graduate of Loughborough and the University of Oregon and a Fulbright Scholar. He is acknowledged as a leading authority in Training Theory and Practice.

A former international athlete himself, he has coached athletes to Olympic, World, European and Commonwealth medals in Decathlon, Hurdles, Javelin, Sprints and High Jump, and is Chief Coach for Relays. He was appointed B.A.F. Director of Coaching in 1979 following 9 years as Scottish National Coach and has lead the United Kingdom's athletics coaching team through a period of unprecedented success in major championships.

This booklet is aimed at teachers, coaches and athletes as a sound basis for understanding the development of athletes in High Jump.

Contents

Photographs

The cover photograph, by courtesy of Mark Shearman, shows Steven Smith (Liverpool H. and G.B.) who cleared 2.37 m in Seoul in 1992 when winning the World Junior Championship. In addition to being a British and Commonwealth Record, this was the highest jump anywhere in the world in 1992 and thus higher than the winning jump at the Olympic Games in Barcelona.

1. Introduction and definition of terms

The name of the game ···

The event is High Jump, and the winner of a high jump competition should be the athlete who is able to jump highest. This apparently self evident observation is overlooked, or rather ignored, whenever *any* of the following are not provided:—

1. A consistent and safe take-off pad. (All-weather, of types such as Tartan, Olymprene, Rubkor, Chevron 440, Resisport, Mondo, etc.)
2. A consistent and safe landing area meeting the following safety standards:—
   Teaching and Club—
        5 m × 2.5 m × 0.55 m
   National/International Competitions—
        5 m × 4 m × 0.65 m
   (Constructed of foam cushions such as those made by Portapit, Lillywhites, Polypit, Kay-Metzeler, Cantabrian etc.)
3. A bar that will not injure the athlete when he hits it or lands on it. This bar will be supported preferably by 2 non-topple uprights.
4. Comfortable and safe footwear offering no possibility of skidding or slipping at take-off.

In other words, the athlete must have no fear of unhappy landings or take-offs. Failure to provide any of the above changes the event from high jump to some sort of survival test.

So the athlete now has all he needs to high jump, and can now accept the challenge: "See that bar up there? Jump over it!" Bearing in mind that it must be a one leg take-off, this is what the athlete will do:—

Verbal description — He runs towards the bar —
Technical terms   (approach run)

Verbal description — crosses over the bar —
Technical terms   (lay-out)

Other technical terms are as follows:—

The leg he jumps from is either his *jumping leg* or *take-off leg*; the non-jumping leg is known as his *free leg*; the limbs nearest the bar at take-off are his *inside limbs* and the others are obviously the *outside limbs*; finally from take-off to landing is known as the athlete's *flight*.

Apologies are made for over-simplification here, but it might help to solve communication problems later!

The athlete quickly understands in this event that there are two objectives to be met, and it is absolutely essential that the objectives are worked for in the order indicated here. To reverse the order of these objectives, or to effect too great a compromise of the first in the interest of safety or lay-out, is the source of every fault in high jump.

First objective

To jump as high as possible from one leg. (APPROACH RUN AND TAKE-OFF).

Second objective

To avoid displacing the bar (lath) used to indicate the height jumped. (LAY-OUT).

The gains in heights jumped at world level have been due primarily to an increase in the athlete's ability to fulfil the first objective rather than the second; yet unfortunately even today the majority of works written extol the virtues of the relative efficiency of one lay-out compared with another. In other words, it is suggested that VALERIY BRUMEL's Straddle began with the first stride of his approach, *not* with the wrapping of his body about the bar; and that DICK FOSBURY's Flop technique began with the

— springs up from the ground —
    (take-off)   (take-off pad)

and lands on the far side of the bar.
(landing)   (landing area)

1

first sprinting stride of his approach, *not* with an arched back over the bar. The improvement of the ladies' event has been quite dramatic since Fosbury introduced to the world *his* fulfilment of our two objectives. However the raising of the standard has not been solely due to his technique. The improvement has come again from work on the first objective, and this has been possibly due to:—

(a) The injury risk being reduced via the development of facilities; in other words, provision of the four items listed above.
(b) Development of those characteristics and techniques necessary for a maximum vertical jump.

Having said all this, it is fairly obvious that the two objectives must be considered as part of the whole jump. The approach and take-off for Brumel's Straddle is quite different from the approach and take-off for Fosbury's Flop. This booklet is set out in such a way that you can examine the fundamentals of the whole jump; see how these have been interpreted; then consider methods of developing the athlete's efficiency relative to the fundamentals via technique and conditioning.

The importance of providing a safe and consistent landing area has already been mentioned. High jumping today would not have reached its present altitude (nor indeed would present-day techniques be possible) without such provision. The event is high jump, and we *must* provide for it. Several authorities have expressed the sentiment that Flop is dangerous and must not be allowed. It is not dangerous, given adequate landing area provision, and is certainly far safer in these circumstances than several variations of tackling on a rugby field; yet no voices have been raised to ban tackling due to latent dangers! Let me conclude by repeating the following quotation from the Committee on the Medical Aspects of Sports of the American Medical Association:—

"It is recognised that all forms of athletic endeavour carry with them the risk of injury. Maximum muscular effort, wide ranges of motion, muscular coordination and flexibility are basic requirements of athletic performance. When performance is according to recommended coaching techniques, the "Fosbury" method of high jumping does not bear greater risks than other methods of high jumping, pole vaulting or gymnastics. It is strongly urged that the rules committee create rules requiring foam rubber or equivalent landing pits for the high jump."

THE FUNDAMENTALS

Like every other athletic event, technique in high jump can be any one of an infinite number of variations on a theme; but the theme *must* have at its core the following fundamental elements.

From start of approach to take-off

1. **The approach run must:—**
   (a) Bring the athlete to a velocity which he can use for an efficient take-off. There should be a rapid increase in speed in the first strides, with a decrease in acceleration over the last three strides. The athlete's smooth and controlled acceleration at the end of the approach must set mind and motor for the jump.
   (b) Bring the athlete to a take-off point that will allow the high point of his jump to be in the plane of the uprights and at the low point of the bar (middle).

At take-off

2. **The take-off foot must:—**
   (a) Be placed in natural alignment with the take-off leg, NOT turned to anticipate rotation.

Diagram 1

(b) Be ahead of the hips and trunk—so that, at the point of take-off, the foot, leg, hip and shoulder on the take-off side are in a vertical and natural alignment. Again it is stressed that this side of the body does *not* create rotation. See diagram 1.

3. The arm(s) must:—

Be vigorously employed by swinging or driving it or them upwards—adding its or their upward momentum to the spring of the take-off leg, whilst holding the shoulder and therefore the trunk in alignment with the hip. When the single arm swing/drive is used it is the *outside* arm.

4. The free leg must:—

(a) Be swung or be driven upwards to add *its* momentum to the spring of the take-off leg. The athlete's own "bio-type" (the type of animal he is) will dictate whether the leg ought to be used bent or straight.

(b) Be used to create long axis rotation (the rotation which a ballet dancer uses in a pirouette).

(c) Be on its way forward *before* the take-off foot is planted, so that the thigh of the free leg is leading the thigh of the take-off leg before it straightens as the take-off leg extends.

5. The take-off leg must:—

Be vigorously and dynamically extended at take-off, to propel the athlete vertically. The efficiency of this action is dependent on the vertical alignment of hip and trunk over take-off leg.

In flight

The athlete must turn and twist his whole body and arrange his limbs in such a way that he or she, at the top of the jump (i.e. over the bar), has no risk of removing the bar with depressed or projecting body parts. In other words, the athlete must aim to make the most of his jump.

Having said this, it is worth looking at some methods which have been used to interpret these fundamentals. However, there have been many more variations and there will surely be other variants in the future.

2. A summary of the most popular methods of high jump

There is more than one way to skin a cat ⋯

Scissors

Very simple and natural—and easily learned by the beginner. It allows considerable use of the free leg and both arms, gets the body efficiently aligned over the take-off foot, but is very inefficient at layout. The jump probably owes much of its appeal to the fact that it allows a landing on the feet—an absolute necessity at earlier points in history, where landing areas were sand or even grass! Fosbury originally did scissors in preference to straddle—but the soft landing area allowed him the variation of landing on his back instead of his feet—and from this very simple situation the Flop developed. See diagram 2.

Flop—Fosbury

Again, very simple and fairly natural, being much easier for the youngster to master than the techniques mentioned below. It allows all the benefits of the scissors take-off but, in the example here, there is a bent free leg used in the interest of a very fast, dynamic take-off. Speed is emphasised in Flop whereas strength is emphasised with the straight leg straddle. The approach run is normally curved so that the athlete places his take-off foot with the body leaning into the curve—as a cyclist does when rounding a tight bend. In other words the shoulders and hips lean *away* from the bar at the moment the athlete places his take-off foot to jump. Moreover, the athlete has reached his take-off foot forward—ahead of hips and shoulders—a fundamental of take-off, so the shoulders and hips are both *behind* the take-off foot, and away from the bar—a situation that is very much in the interest of a subsequent efficient vertical spring. See diagram 3.

Diagram 2

Diagram 3

In all these "Flops" we've seen one similar pattern after take-off. The athlete pulls the heels back under the body as he tries to "lift" the hips over the bar in a feat of exceptional back mobility. Once the hips are over, the athlete tucks or pikes at the middle to flip the legs over. (See sequences 1, 2, 3, and 4. Pages 8/15).

Eastern cut-off

There are several similarities existing between the Scissors, the Flop and this technique, which was developed on the Eastern seaboard of the United States (hence its title). All employ a take-off from the outside leg, and all are relatively simple methods of obtaining a sound take-off, employing most if not all of our fundamentals. That is where it stops, however, because Eastern Cut-Off, like all other techniques except Flop, had to be developed with a poor landing area in mind.

The lay-out is quite economical, but still falls short of the efficiency of Flop or Straddle. However, like Scissors, it illustrates a method of interpreting our fundamentals—and although one would not recommend it to today's high jumper as a technique worth developing, there can be no argument against its use as a training variant. See diagram 4.

Western Roll

So the Western seaboard of the United States had to add its name to a technique. Both Eastern and Western techniques could be described as hopping over the bar; Eastern from the outside foot—demanding, if nothing else, a formidable piece of agility in the recovery of the jumping leg; and the Western from the inside foot. For years teaching drills were developed for hopping over canes or bars to a "three point landing". No three point landing meant no Western roll, and no Western roll meant no more high jump to thousands of youngsters, for "scissors" jumpers were normally advised to "forget" it, Western roll being

Diagram 4

Diagram 5

5

more "mechanically sound" over the bar. Again the emphasis, you see, was on a safe landing. However, the event is *high* jumping—not mastery of a flight or landing technique. Several athletes claimed great success in the event using a Western roll in preference to Straddle. As with Eastern Cut-Off, this lay-out technique is not one which should be developed—but of course it offers another piece of variety in the training session. See diagram 5.

Straddle

But without doubt, the greatest advances in high jump accompanied the development of Straddle, and the greatest work ever written on high jump, "High Jumping" by Professor V.M. DYATCHKOV, set down the only truth—that high jumping is performed on the ground. Through clouds of confusion about where legs, head and hands were in flight came a shaft of light that detailed distance, speed, technique of running in the approach, preparations for take-off, take-off itself, and development of all these. Together with Flop, Straddle will continue to raise the world standards—but only when Flop and Straddle are considered as total jumps, from the start of the approach to bar clearance. Speed and elasticity of muscle is to bent free leg Flop as momentum and strength of muscle contraction is to straight free leg Straddle. As you examine the sequence of ROLF BEILSCHMIDT look for his interpretation of our fundamentals. (See Sequence 5 on Pages 16/17).

Just as there were variations in Flop, so also in Straddle. Remember that this technique started in the 30's when landing areas were less safe than today—so some consideration had to be given to landing techniques and this was reflected in lay-out. Also, the principle underlying the use of a straight free leg has been weighed against the use of a fast bent free leg, as in some versions of the Flop. There are athletes more suited to bent knee Straddle because, like the Flops, it calls for characteristic of speed of muscle contraction rather than strength of muscle contraction. Their "bio-type" is very similar to that of the long jumper—an athlete who gets great spring from only a brief contact time with the ground. The point being made here is that you must select a technique to which a given athlete is suited.

In Sequence 7 PAT MATZDORF demonstrates a bent knee Straddle, yet puts together the fundamentals of take-off we have discussed already. Once in flight, he has the same problem as all Straddlers—he must revolve round the bar, yet keep his hips from the bar and lift his free leg clear. As you can see from this sequence, his method of doing this is different from that used by Beilschmidt or Ackermann. (See Sequences 6 and 7 on Pages 18/20).

It is not suggested that the foregoing describe all the possible high jump techniques. After all, Fosbury developed his interpretation of the fundamentals from scratch; there were no books nor diagrams to which he could refer, nor coaches to advise him. It is more than likely that there are further avenues to be explored, *but* all must embrace the suggested fundamentals if they are to be successful.

ATHLETICS COACH

THE COACHING BULLETIN OF THE B.A.F.

Published:

March, June, September, December

Details from:

Malcolm Arnold
56 Rolls Avenue
Penpedairheol
Hengoed, Mid. Glam. CF8 8HQ

GRT 6

GRT 5

GRT 4

GRT 12

GRT 11

GRT 10

GRT 15

GRT 14

GRT 13

GRT 3   GRT 2   GRT 1

GRT 9   GRT 8   GRT 7

Each athlete in the sequences illustrated in this book has his or her individual interpretation of technique. Each has developed what fits his or her strengths and weaknesses. The final product is, then, a picture of unique compensations within a framework of biomechanical principles. DALTON GRANT shows aggressive sprinting (GRT 1, 3), yet employs a two arm technique at take-off (GRT 7, 8, 9). Here, he steps out of the curve (GRT 6) creating a problem—yet corrects alignment of body parts to produce an effective take-off (GRT 7, 8, 9). Bar clearance, however, is the most extraordinary set of compensations. Few athletes have such capacity to perform so many adjustments with such time and space commitments! (GRT 10–14).

Sequence 2

HH 6

HH 5

HH 4

HH 12

HH 11

HH 10

HH 16

HH 15

HH 14

HH 3

HH 2

HH 1

HH 9

HH 8

HH 7

HH 13

Rotations in flight have their preconditions set in the approach and take-off. The more time an athlete has in flight (ie. the higher they are jumping), the less emphatic are those movements to create the preconditions. HEIKE HENKEL does not *need* to work so hard for rotation about the vertical axis; note left foot (HE 8, 9). For many athletes this would substantially reduce efficiency of take-off. However, Heike Henkel is exceptional in the early and fast pull through of her thigh (see HE 5, 6, 7, 8)—and she gets the lift she needs. Also note shoulders turning away from the bar (HE 4, 5, 6, 7, 8).

Sequence 3

SI 6

SI 5

SI 4

SI 12

SI 11

SI 10

SI 17

SI 16

SI 15

SI 3

SI 2

SI 1

SI 9

SI 8

SI 7

In the development of this technique there has been an increasing emphasis on take-off efficiency. SARA SIMEONI shows well the setting of her hips and shoulders during the stride into take-off. In many ways this is simply applying a lesson learned in straddle—and underlines that certain elements are fundamental to all technical variations. Simeoni has used her inside arm to help set the shoulders and avoid inside shoulder drop at take-off. Any momentum contribution comes from the action of the outside arm.

SI 14

SI 13

Sequence 4

GR 6　　　GR 5　　　GR 4

GR 12　　　GR 11　　　GR 10

GR 17　　　GR 16　　　GR 15

GR 3

GR 2

GR 1

GR 9

GR 8

GR 7

The lifeblood of technical development is experimentation in interpretation of basic principles. GRIGOREYEV demonstrates his interpretation of blending elements of classical straddle take-off, and flop clearance. Note the use of both arms plus straight leg swing to maximise the component of momentum in take-off.

GR 14

GR 13

BE 1   BE 2   BE 3

BE 7   BE 8   BE 9

BE 13   BE 14   BE 15

BE 4

BE 5

BE 6

BE 10

BE 11

BE 12

BEILSCHMIDT's technique is a modern classic straddle. He emphasises acceleration into take-off.

BE 16

BE 17

AC 1   AC 2   AC 3

AC 7   AC 8   AC 9

AC 13   AC 14   AC 15

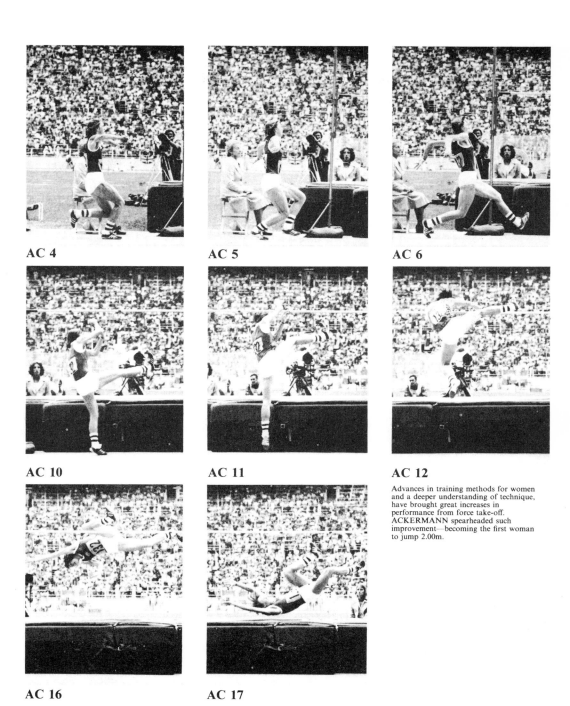

AC 4

AC 5

AC 6

AC 10

AC 11

AC 12

Advances in training methods for women
and a deeper understanding of technique,
have brought great increases in
performance from force take-off.
ACKERMANN spearheaded such
improvement—becoming the first woman
to jump 2.00m.

AC 16

AC 17

Sequence 7 PAT MATZDORF

3. Explanation of take-off and approach run variations. The origins of rotation

The age of ascent

Take-off and approach

To recap—these two aspects of the total jump are the only aspects which contribute to achievement of our first objective, "to jump as high as possible from one leg". So this chapter is of critical importance to both coach and athlete.

Just as moving into the basic, balanced throwing position and subsequent synchronizing of movements is the key-stone in discus throwing, so moving into the basic, balanced jumping position and synchronizing subsequent movements is fundamental to jumping. We should, therefore, consider take-off first, and then consider the approach to take-off.

There are two basic take-off techniques used:—
- (a) The momentum/strength take-off (where great strength is applied with less velocity)
  = STRENGTH × velocity
- (b) The impulse/velocity take-off (where less strength is applied with great velocity)
  = strength × VELOCITY

The extreme example of the former is the straight-leg straddle take-off as employed by Brumel. It is suggested that the contact time at the take-off foot lies within the range of 0.18-0.22 sec. An ability to sustain the expression of force is therefore implied and such a technique is only for the strong athlete. The development potential in such a technique is great, when one considers that strength, as a physical characteristic, can be considerably increased by relevant training methods.

The extreme example of the latter is the flop take-off as employed by Fosbury. Its similarity to long jump take-off extends beyond the visual aspect since the contact time of the take-off foot with the flop lies in the range of 0.13-0.15 sec. and that of long jump 0.10-0.12 sec. To emphasise the point, it should be noted that the foot contact time of a sprinter is 0.08 sec. In other words, it is the take-off for the athlete with the gift of speed. Since the characteristic of speed *of knee extension* can be improved only minimally through training, compared with strength, there is an implied limitation to ultimate jumping potential with this type of take-off, unless great emphasis is placed on "elastic strength" or power, i.e. the ability to express force at speed. However, there is still considerable velocity increase of coordinated limb movement possible before maximum is reached. To summarise, there is the possibility of high jump improvement by developing strength, and/or velocity and/or elastic strength.

To understand these points, we must accept that the two types of take-off are suited to two types of human animal, or two different "bio-types".

That these two types exist is beyond doubt, but identification of type as a basis for selection of technique for an individual athlete creates a problem for the following reasons:—
1. Hettinger states "the percentage of elasticity is higher than strength" in woman; this "types" the woman for the second take-off.
2. Vittori states "that they (boys) are only prepared for classical (Brumel) straddle at the age of 15-16 years".
3. Strength as a physical characteristic is best developed in the maturing rather than the growing organism—indicating that strength events are for the late teens and twenties.

Taking all these facts, it would appear that the "velocity take-off" is more relevant to the woman and young athlete, and that conversely the "strength take-off" is only for the exceptions in these groups. Why is this a problem? Because the learning of the force take-off may well be omitted in pursuit of high performance in the young and the female, and when the "bio-type" finally *does* become evident, or when strength is acquired, the athlete may be too committed to the velocity take-off. The solution? Ensure that the young high jumper learns both types of take-off, so that when a mature athlete he or she will be able to use the best technique for him or her.

The next question is clearly "How can one identify these two types?" Until such time as a fool-proof test has been devised, the best rule of thumb would appear to be to isolate the "velocity take-off" athlete by looking at his or her other events. You will probably find him or her to be a useful sprinter, long jumper or hurdler. Although some good "strength take-off" men have recorded excellent high hurdles times, it is suggested that this is more closely related to specific hip mobility and leg strength than to speed, so double check the hurdler-high jumper by looking at long jump efficiency (velocity take-off) and standing vertical/sargent jump efficiency (strength take-off).

Whatever the athlete's apparent bio-type and the development route prepared by the coach, it remains a truism that the athlete who jumps highest is best equipped to apply most force in the shortest period of time. Consequently, *all* athletes must work on improvement of all round, maximum and elastic strength, and learn to apply this at speed. It is at this point that coaches appreciate the need for a harmonious marriage of conditioning and technique work.

The strength take-off

The take-off foot is placed far ahead of the body, and the line of the leg-hip-trunk is drawn back from the vertical. The "placing"

of the take-off foot is the result of a dynamic downwards and backwards striking action of the take-off leg. The heel lands first but is immediately followed by the whole foot slapping on to the take-off surface. At this point the athlete feels as if his body weight is being directed through the foot at a point just behind the ball of the foot. The load on the muscles of the take-off leg is considerable, and the knee, of course, is obliged to flex —yielding to the load. Great strength is necessary to complete an efficient take-off from such a position, and the duration of strength application in the take-off phase is necessarily relatively long. This type of take-off might also be referred to as the momentum-transfer take-off, since, used to optimal effect, the straight free leg and both arms are vigorously employed to add lift. However, in order to co-ordinate this take-off leg extension, and to bring the arms and the free leg to a synchronised and efficient conclusion, the various components must be "set" in position before and as the take-off foot is planted.

The sequence of movements involved in this setting are as follows:—

1. Both arms are held in front of the body and are medially rotated—thumbs turned in, elbows out.
2. (a) The arms are now drawn back with elbows at shoulder height, not only to prepare the arms for a wide range of momentum development but also, and more importantly, to hold the shoulders and therefore the trunk in position while the hips are "rolled" under and ahead of shoulders and trunk.
   (b) The horizontal velocity of the approach run pushes the weight of the body over the free leg, *which never straightens* in this stride, on to the take-off foot. In fact it should be used as a sound rule of thumb that from

the time the body weight passes over the free leg—until the moment that the thigh of the free leg is drawn level with that of the take-off leg—the angle at the knee and at the ankle is never greater than 90°.

(c) The take-off leg is brought through naturally, without any exaggerated knee lift.

3. (a) The elbows are brought to the limits of their backward movement.

(b) The hips are rolled under and ahead of the trunk and shoulders.

(c) The take-off leg reaches for a heel first landing, drawing the hip forward. This fast heel-sole plant must *not* be a jarring/braking action.

From this point a successful take-off can proceed.

But it can only proceed to a successful conclusion given the following sequence.
1. Free hip drives forward and upward.
2. Free leg accelerates forward and upwards, drawn by the hip—as a whip handle draws the lash. The combined action of free leg acceleration forwards and upwards, and take-off leg strike downwards and backwards may be thought of as a "scissoring" of the legs.
3. (a) Both arms chase and ultimately match the velocity of the free leg.

(b) The take-off leg completes a vigorous extension as arms and free leg complete their lift.

(See Sequence 5 of Beilschmidt 6-10. Pages 16/17)

Velocity take-off

The take-off foot is not reached out as far ahead of the body as in the strength take-off (1), nor is there such an emphatic move of leg, hip, trunk, shoulder alignment from the vertical (2). See diagram 1.

In addition it can be clearly seen that there is a difference in trunk/shoulder alignment with hip/leg.

Reasons for these differences are fairly obvious. If you can imagine the athlete approaching the take-off at speed; in order to synchronise take-off, the athlete must set the trunk relative to hip in such a way that the knee extension does not precede the arrival of hip and trunk *over* the take-off foot, and yet offers the additional force of hip extension. This type of take-off, then, requires the athlete to carry his weight towards the balls of the feet even in his 3rd and 2nd last strides, presenting a heel/flat foot only at take-off. This implies less time over the take-off foot to generate vertical lift, involving a lesser maximum angle of flexion in the take-off knee than in straddle. (See Sequence 7 of Matzdorf 11-15, on Page 20)

Returning to a point mentioned earlier, the characteristic of the strength take-off is the development of lift by transfer of momentum of swinging parts of the body, emphasising the component of strength of force expression, while the velocity take-off is the development of lift emphasising the component of *velocity* of force expression.

Without doubt, the velocity take-off is much easier to learn, since the co-ordination of other limbs for momentum transfer is not, in the simplest form, essential. However, the arms are certainly used to "set" the shoulders and trunk in position over the hips.

Sequence 3 Simeoni 7-10, on Pages 12/13

The action necessary for this can range from that used for the strength take-off, to merely feeling the position of the shoulders just as the long jumper does, Whatever happens, the trunk must not fold forward over the hips, nor must the take-off knee advance ahead of the toes. Both of these points can be clearly observed by the coach.

Sequence 1 Grant 7-9 on Pages 8/9

Sequence 2 Henkel 6-9 on Pages 10/11

SA 1

SA 2

SA 3

SA 4

KESTUTIS SAPKA *U.S.S.R.*

Irrespective of total technique, the basic principles of jumping must be followed.

Sequence 3 Simeoni 8-10 on Pages 12/13

Sequence 7 Matzdorf 12-16 on Page 20

Sequence 8 Sapka 1-4 on Page 24

So while it is insisted that this is a simple and natural take-off, great care must be taken that the sprinting action of the approach does not encroach upon the take-off, giving a sloppy and therefore flat take-off. The key should be for the athlete to imagine that he or she is trying to walk tall up steps, with a glass of water on the crown of his or her head. The free foot is always behind the free knee during take-off, *both* shoulders are shrugged or hunched upwards, and the hips are pressed forward and upward, irrespective of the layout that is to succeed this take-off.

In summary, the sequence of action is:—

1. Set shoulders and trunk.
2. Free hip drives forward and upward.
3. Complete extension of ankle, knee and hip drives head and shoulders vertically.

Approach run for strength take-off

It should be said that to date the most efficient interpretation of a strength take-off is built on a straight approach run, as in Brumel straddle. (See Beilschmidt Sequence 5 and Ackermann Sequence 6.)

The running pattern of the approach must rapidly accelerate the athlete *before* he arrives at the last three strides, where a decrease in acceleration will provide the biokinetic conditions for the transfer of horizontal to vertical lift. Whether or not the strength take-off jumper has run on his heels up to this point, these last three strides are, generally speaking, made on the heel or flat footed—and the athlete settles in preparation for the jump.

Sequences 5 & 6 on Pages 16/19

The total number of strides employed in the approach is fairly arbitrary but, discounting preliminary sways, walks, skips, etc., 7-9 strides are common for the straight approach.

The direction of the take-off relative to the bar is critical and must, of course, be dictated by the approach. For the strength take-off from the inside foot, the angle between the direction of take-off and the bar is dictated by:—

(a) The distance from take-off to the high point of the jump (which should be at the low point of the bar—the centre).
(b) The space required by an athlete to prevent horizontal velocity carrying the rising free leg into the bar.

As a rule of thumb from which you may adjust to suit the athlete—try this.

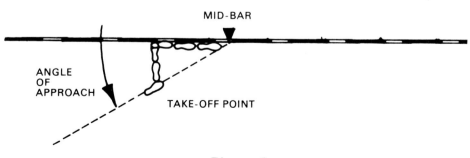

Diagram 6

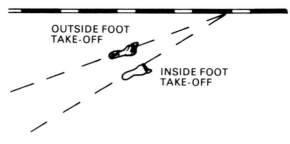

Diagram 7

For the strength take-off from the outside foot, while the same factors dictate approach angle, the greatest problem exists with the rising free leg. In this event, the angle of approach should be made more acute. (See diagram 7).

By doing this there would be considerable travel along the bar unless there was a second horizontal component carrying the athlete toward the bar. How can such a horizontal velocity be given to the athlete, without the athlete giving himself an eccentric force that will tilt him at the bar?

One answer to this problem was provided by Fosbury when he used an outside leg velocity take-off from a curved approach.

Approach for a velocity take-off

Before Fosbury introduced this idea, the velocity take-off had also been approached in a straight line, but the pattern of the run was slightly different from that of the orthodox strength take-off. There was a gradual increase in velocity throughout the run, with an active and positive acceleration over the last three strides. Whilst this might be seen as an alternative approach-run pattern, it should be noted that few coaching authorities recommend its use.

Returning to the problem posed above, let us examine how Fosbury solved it with the curve for a velocity take-off and discuss its suitability for a strength take-off. To run a curve it is necessary for an athlete to lean his body inwards—toward the centre of the circle he is describing. He will also be moving in a definite direction round this circle, clockwise or anti-clockwise. Diagram 8 shows what we would see if we had an aerial view of him running in a clockwise direction.

Notice that while this general course might be described as circular, he progresses by a series of straight lines representing each stride.

You will notice that, because of this lean, his head describes a smaller circle than his feet.

Two situations of great significance occur as consequences.

1. As he comes in to take-off from his curved approach, he is therefore leaning away from the bar. This will:—

   (i) Give extra time over the take-off foot.

   (ii) Give time and space for the free leg to be used without endangering the bar.

   (iii) Initiate a rotation into the bar before the vigorous extension when the body reaches the vertical.

   (iv) With (ii), give a flight direction involving less travel along the bar.

2. Also, due to the setting of his shoulders and slight forward reach of his take-off foot, his hips and trunk are displaced behind the take-off foot. So he jumps from this position which:—

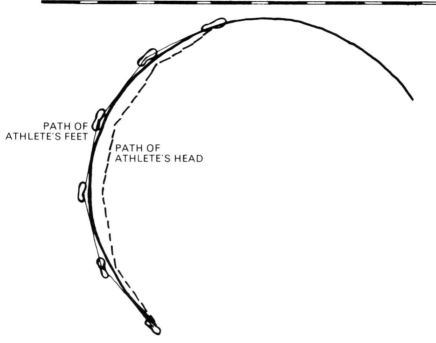

PATH OF
ATHLETE'S FEET

PATH OF
ATHLETE'S HEAD

Diagram 8

(i) Gives time proportionate to the type of take-off, for optimal vertical lift.

(ii) With 1, gives the flight direction described in 1 (iv).

(iii) By drawing the free knee towards the take-off hip, and by keeping his shoulders square to the direction of running, a rotation is initiated about the long axis. (This movement also pulls the "dangerous" free leg *away* from the bar). See diagram 9.

This means quite simply that the athlete has given himself:—

(i) An efficient velocity take-off.

(ii) Two types of rotation; one that will let him go over the bar on his back, and a second that will enable him to do so head first.

It should be clearly understood that for the advantages of the curved approach to exist, only the last three strides of the approach need be on a curve. In other words— although Fosbury used 8 strides, all on the curve, it is feasible that the first 5 could have

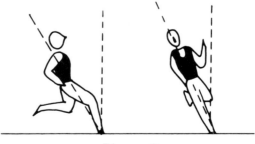

Diagram 9

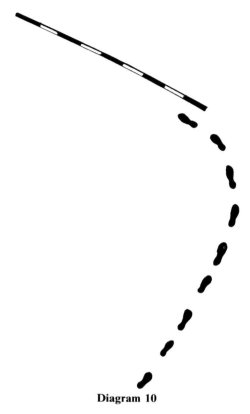

Diagram 10

been straight and the last 3 on a curve, with the approach assuming the shape of a walking stick or "J". See diagram 10.

There is less of a problem of moulding a curved approach to a velocity take-off from the *inside* foot. In fact, if the athlete is well enough co-ordinated, it could prove of some value in affording a little more time over the take-off foot. The result will be a form of dive straddle.

The question now arises, can the curved approach be combined with a strength take-off—and would there be an advantage gained in doing so?

There has, in fact, been experimentation in this area, using both inside and outside foot take-offs. There are problems of course, but these are not insurmountable.

From the outside foot: *There has already been successful experimentation here.*

(See Sequence 8 Sapka 1-4 on Page 24).

The fact that the athlete is leaning away from the free leg side might be seen as an advantage as it will allow an earlier straightening of that leg. However, there are injury risks in the medial eccentric loading of the take-off knee and ankle, and the possible pulling of free leg adductors and medial rotators.

From the inside foot: *there are considerable difficulties here:—*

(a) The athlete will have a big problem in how to use efficiently a straight free leg, since he would be leaning to that side.
(b) While the curved run will favour a long axis rotation of his body away from the bar, the swing of his free leg will favour rotation towards the bar.
(c) The nett result here, then, is that the take-off is at a much wider angle to the bar than with other techniques. (See Mracnova—Sequence 9 on Pages 38/39).
(d) Balance and co-ordination problems are greater than for orthodox straight approach Straddle.

Rotations at take-off

For as long as the athlete's take-off foot is in contact with the ground, all rotations will take place about axes acting through the foot. See diagram 11.

It is very useful in describing rotations to indicate the direction as clockwise or anti-clockwise. See diagram 12.

The rotations given to the body at take-off are due:—

(a) To the free leg being swung upwards or pulled across the body. This causes rotation about the long axis and rotates the athlete towards the side opposite the swung or pulled leg, i.e. if the right leg is

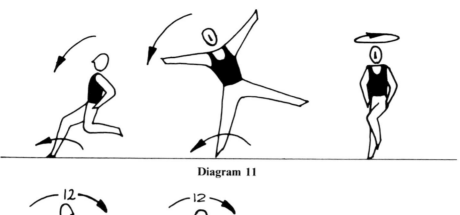

Diagram 11

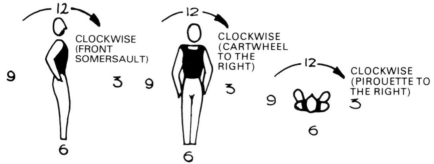

Diagram 12

the free leg, it will rotate the athlete anti-clockwise. *Such rotations must never come from the take-off leg.*

(b) To the body's sideways displacement of weight. This causes rotation about the anterio-posterior axis. It is not to be encouraged, unless by natural process of the body straightening to the vertical from the "lean-in" of the athlete who uses a curved approach. The rotation having been created in this way must not cause the athlete's inside shoulder to dip into the bar. Again such rotation must never come from the take-off leg. See diagram 13.

(c) To the body's forward or backward displacement of weight. This causes rotation about the transverse axis—and it is this type of rotation that the athlete is at pains to minimise. This rotation is,

29

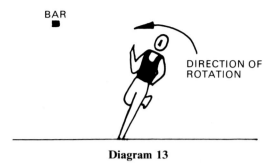

BAR

DIRECTION OF ROTATION

Diagram 13

however, a natural outcome of the straightening of the body to the vertical over the take-off leg.

Bearing all this in mind, you will quickly see that the athlete who takes off from his inside foot will rotate quite naturally about the long axis to *face* the bar (e.g. Straddle type jump), whereas the athlete who takes-off from his outside foot will rotate quite naturally about the long axis to present his back to the bar (e.g. Flop type jump).

This topic is included at this point in the booklet, together with take-off and approach, to emphasise that lay-out techniques grow from consideration of the approach take-off and associated rotation. In other words, the athlete's preference for a strength or velocity take-off must be established first; *then* the preference for inside or outside foot for take-off, *then* the preference for flight techniques.

By way of summary, the efficiency of take-off is related to the nature of the approach run; and the implied lay-out technique is related to the nature and direction of rotations created at take-off, by total body movement about the take-off foot, or by the use of the free limbs, but not from the take-off leg itself.

TABLE 1

APPROACH	COURSE	TAKE-OFF TYPE	TAKE-OFF LEG	LAY-OUT
7-9	STRAIGHT*	STRENGTH	INSIDE	STRADDLE
7-9	STRAIGHT§	VELOCITY	INSIDE	STRADDLE
8-10	CURVED§	VELOCITY	INSIDE	STRADDLE
8-10	CURVED*	STRENGTH	OUTSIDE	FLOP
8-10	CURVED§	VELOCITY	OUTSIDE	FLOP
8-10	STRAIGHT*	VELOCITY	OUTSIDE	FLOP

* Fast start with reduced acceleration but increased stride frequency over the last 3 strides.
§ Gradual acceleration throughout, with increased acceleration and stride frequency over the last 3 strides.

4. Biomechanics of Vertical Spring

Groundwork is soundwork

The previous chapter answered the question "how?" with reference to approach and take-off. To answer the question "why?", we must return to bio-mechanics.

Bio-mechanics of vertical spring

Of all the factors involved in executing a perfect high jump, the entry into take-off from the approach is the most important. The approach run velocity can only be of value if such velocity, and the manner of loading it onto the take-off leg, can be used by the athlete to benefit take-off efficiency. To help understand the problem, one must turn to the bio-mechanics of this situation.

If an athlete performs a standing vertical jump, he bends his knees, pauses and *then* extends the knees vigorously to spring from the ground: there are two actions—one of bending the knees, then a new one of extending them. In other words, the purpose of bending the knees is to put himself in a starting position from which to jump. If the same athlete takes off from one step, and still takes off from both feet, he can increase the height jumped by 15-20 cm. This time there is an instantaneous change in movement direction. Knees bend with the impact of the "fall" of the body weight onto the legs from the preparatory step and immediately extend again—the whole movement being like that of a ball, bouncing.

With the first jump the athlete merely gives himself a range through which to extend his knees, whilst in the second some elastic property of the muscle seems to be involved. Such a mechanism must have some considerable value to the athlete, so it deserves further investigation.

Let's go back to the ball! If a ball is dropped onto a concrete floor, the following factors will determine how high it will bounce:—

1. The angle at which the ball strikes the floor. All things being equal, a vertical drop will produce an optimal height of vertical bounce.
2. The height from which the ball falls. The greater the height, the greater the velocity of the ball when it strikes the floor, and the greater the height of the rebound.
3. The elasticity of the ball. The more elastic, the quicker and more forceful will be its return to its original round shape following its distortion on impact with the ground. Thus, for example, we have "slow" or "fast" squash balls.

Putting these three factors together, the velocity developed by the falling ball gives it energy to bounce—(2). Such energy is referred to as kinetic energy because it is obtained from the movement of the ball. Provided the ball is dropped vertically—(1), and is of very elastic material—(3), the kinetic energy will be efficiently used to give the ball the highest vertical bounce possible.

But of course the athlete is a much more complex mechanism than a ball, and he has the problem of using the kinetic energy of a horizontal approach to give vertical "bounce".

Unfortunately there is a danger that the coach and athlete might think of this change of direction as similar to the standing vertical jump situation, but this is most certainly not the case. It is not a horizontal run, a pause, then a vertical spring; but the creating of kinetic energy, which must be efficiently used for vertical spring by calling upon the elastic properties of muscle in the jumping leg. Just as the surface of the ball "resists" being flattened, so the unlocked jumping knee resists being bent further. At this juncture it seems propitious to explain exactly how the muscle can develop the elastic properties necessary for greater efficiency in using the kinetic energy of the approach for vertical spring. There are three essential factors which dictate this efficiency:—

1. The muscle that extends the knee (quadriceps) must be tensed *before* the kinetic energy of the approach is loaded onto it. Of course, this knee of the jumping leg must not be locked when the take-off foot lands—otherwise there can be no elastic effect and only a terrible jarring of the athlete's body, bringing him to a rapid halt and introducing a big injury risk. The loading of the take-off leg caused by the athlete's approach velocity and, depending on take-off momentum of arms and free leg—forces the take-off knee to bend—thus "stretching the elastic" or "compressing the spring". The degree of flexion varies from 140°-148° in bent free leg Flop to 135°-142° in classic straight free leg Straddle. Should the flexion angles become less than these values, then the kinetic energy of the approach is absorbed and wasted, because the athlete does not have the strength to use it and therefore cannot benefit from the elastic effect.

2. As the muscle is being stretched "against its will", a mechanism is brought into play that causes it to contract powerfully. This is a very special reflex action called the **MYOTONIC REFLEX**, and is well known in throwing the discus or javelin.

3. The athlete consciously extends the knee powerfully to spring into the air. Remember that in the final analysis it is the athlete who determines the amount of force with which he will spring from the ground. It is he who co-ordinates the whole movement—setting his body for the jump, tensing the muscles of the take-off leg and exploding upwards from the ground.

This understood, there now seems little problem. We must now simply train the athlete to co-ordinate these three factors

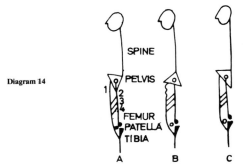

Diagram 14

A	B	C
PELVIS TILTED: UPWARDS	DOWNWARDS	NORMAL
RECTUS FEMORIS: STRETCHED	SLACK	NORMAL

Diagram 14

through frequent practices. From (3)—we encourage the athlete to approach fast, and pretense the extensors of the take-off leg (1); then reflex contraction (2), the elastic recoil of the muscle (1) and concentrated dynamic extension by the athlete will ensure a good jump. However, things can still go wrong if the athlete is not co-ordinating the take-off movement correctly. Fortunately there is still one final key to the problem. That key is provided by kinesiology—the study of movement. The diagram of the spine, hip, knee and ankle is a schematic representation of the vital area in question. See diagram 14.

The muscle which straightens the knee is called the quadriceps (four heads), because it has four heads. It also has one tail which is attached to a bone called the tibia below the knee. You can see that three heads are attached to the femur (2, 3, 4) and one is attached to the pelvis (1). If the athlete plants his take-off foot and holds his spine and pelvis as in (a), then all four heads of the quadriceps can be tensed and therefore used to the athlete's advantage.

Moreover as weight passes over the extending take-off leg, there is a sound alignment of the body parts to enable the athlete to thrust his body vertically from the take-off leg. On the other hand, if the spine and hip are set as in (B), it is impossible to tense

The synchronised rolling under of the pelvis is helped by two distinct actions of the athlete.

and use the "head" that is attached to the hip (1), and the body parts are aligned in such a way that vertical thrust will be absorbed and the jump wasted.

At first reading you may think that all of this is academic, but the key to the athlete using the kinetic energy of the approach to give vertical spring does lie here. The moment that the heel of the take-off foot makes contact with the ground, the athlete must accelerate the hip forward with a very distinct and forceful movement. The movement is not only that of the whole pelvis shifting forward, but of rolling the pelvis under. He should feel that the lower part of the pelvis is pressing forwards and upwards, while the top of his pelvis is pressing backwards and downwards.

1. The holding back of the shoulders, with elbows out, draws the spine (trunk) back.

2. The free leg knee *never* fully extends as it pushes the athlete onto his take-off foot. The athlete "rocks" over the free leg as he makes his last step prior to take-off. The limit of flexion in this "rocking" action ranges from 125°-138° (velocity take-off) to 90°-98° (strength take-off)—and the degree of extension of the knee at push-off onto the take-off leg ranges from 160°-170° (velocity take-off) to 90°-110° (strength take-off). This action accelerates the hip forward into an ideal alignment of trunk-hip-take-off leg. Not only does this action aid the jumping efficiency of the take-off leg, but it also assists the rapid drawing forward of the free thigh. Hence the coaching point of emphasising a scissoring action of the legs into take-off; or a pulling "through and up" of the hip. Finally, in a straight leg strength take-off, since the original swing of the free leg is downwards and forwards, there is an increased loading of the tensed take-off quadriceps through transfer of momentum. Thus the kinetic energy of the approach run is added to by the momentum transfer of the free leg, but only if the movement forward of the free thigh is fast.

Sequence 5 (5-9, on Pages 16/17).
Sequence 6 (7-10, on Pages 18/19).

By way of summary; the athlete creates kinetic energy with the velocity of his approach, and sets his hips to allow the development of tension in the extensors of the take-off knee. The elastic recoil from the increased tension, combined with a vigorous reflex action and the co-ordinated dynamic expression of extension on the part of the athlete, will produce an optimal height of vertical jump.

5. Flight and Layout

Should I react to Isaac, and will things take a turn for the better?

If a gymnast performs a cartwheel across the floor, his means of progression are immediately apparent to the onlooker. The gymnast's entire body rotates over the hand in contact with the floor until the other hand reaches the floor. The body then rotates over that hand until a foot lands; then rotates over the foot until the other foot reaches the floor, and so on. In other words, progression of the body along the floor is the result of the body rotating about that part which is on the floor. See diagram 15.

So also for a tyre rolled along the road, progression is achieved by the same process. In summary, then, any rotation of the whole body whilst it still has contact with the ground, must take place about an axis through the part in contact with the ground (foot) or fixed point (e.g. gymnast's hands on a high bar). This fact has already been touched upon when we discussed rotation at take-off. Now let's imagine the tyre rolling along the ground, then up a short ramp, and finally flying through the air. See diagram 16.

The wheel cannot now rotate about a point in contact with the ground because it is in flight. Nevertheless it is rotating as it flies. Now the rotation is about the hub or centre of the wheel and not its rim. If you think about it, the hub is the centre of the wheel's weight, no matter which way you look at it, and such a point must exist in all bodies —whether they are wheels, balls, boxes, pyramids or athletes. This point is referred to as the "centre of gravity" of a body, and no matter how the body rotates and twists in flight, the centre of gravity will always describe that curve in flight dictated by the speed and angle of launching or take-off.

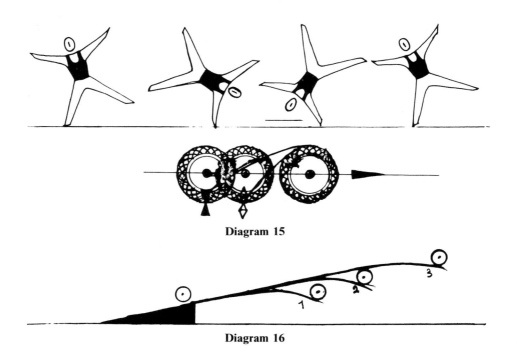

Diagram 15

Diagram 16

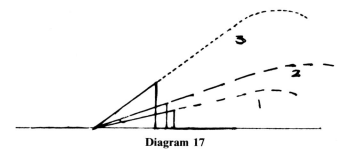

Diagram 17

Thus the centre of gravity of our wheel will describe the short curve (1) if the approach speed is slow; the longer and higher curve (2) if the approach speed is faster; and the very long curve (3) if the approach is faster still.

Keeping the speed of the approach the same and altering the angle of the launching pad will have a similar effect. See diagram 17.

You can see how the height of the curve has been raised from (1) to (3). In some articles you will see the flight curves referred to as a "parabola of flight" because of its symmetry. Why is it symmetrical? Because as the centre of gravity rises along the flight curve, it is being pulled back to earth by the same force (gravity)—throughout.

Both the velocity of approach and the steepness of the "launching angle" are therefore responsible for the shape of the parabola of flight. You should understand this in order to understand the "flight" aspect of the jump. Obviously the approach velocity of the athlete relates directly to that of the wheel, but the athlete must create his own launching angle by those methods suggested in discussing the linking of approach run to take-off. In high jump the athlete must strive for the highest possible parabola of flight, derived from a steep angle to take-off and efficient use of the kinetic energy of the approach. The highest point of the parabola must be directly over the bar and at the lowest point of the bar—the centre. The actual take-off point must therefore be carefully calculated to ensure this. The coach can easily see this by observing the jump from two positions. See diagram 18.

If from (1) the coach sees the high point of the jump *before* the bar, then the take-off is too far from the bar. If from (2) the coach sees the high point to his left (lined area),

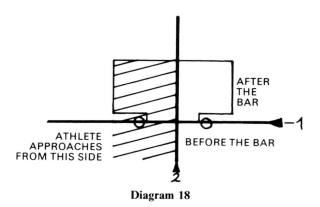

Diagram 18

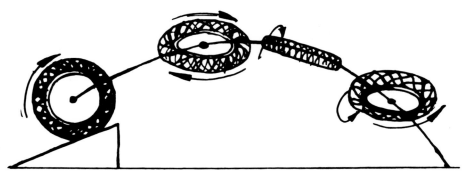

Diagram 19

then the take-off is too early. Adjustments will then be made by bringing the starting point of the approach run further forward. The converse would be true if the athlete is too close at take-off.

Let us return to the tyre running up its small ramp, and let us imagine that it is tipped sideways at take-off. It will still have its normal forward "rolling" action in flight, *but* there will now be an additional rotation causing it to turn over on its side. If we watched this from the side, this is what we would see happen. See diagram 19.

So the tyre is now rotating about two axes; yet the parabola of flight remains symmetrical, established by approach velocity and angle of launching. Rotation about the third axis would still not interfere with this parabola; in fact in the example set out, rotation about the third axis would be a consequence of rotation about the other two axes. Why is that? Well, although it is of interest only, at this juncture, it does emphasise the point being made. The third rotation would be due to the law or principle of PRECESSION:—If a body is rotating clockwise about one axis, and a force causes it to rotate clockwise about a second axis, the body will react by rotating clockwise about a third axis. (Conversely, if anti-clockwise about the second axis, the reaction is also anti-clockwise. Clock "faces" are as described in rotation at take-off—diagram 12).

Time has been spent on the subject of rotation and on the concept of the parabola of flight to emphasise:—

1. That the flight path of the centre of gravity is fixed at take-off.
2. That rotation is initiated at take-off (not by the take-off leg).
3. That direct and indirect rotations are possible in flight, as a consequence of (2).
4. That three axes of rotation are "available".
5. In addition to rotation, certain action/reaction movements are possible in flight—e.g. piking.

The variety of shapes, twists and speeds of rotation possible in flight is vast—but learning how to control the body in flight may rest more in the area of the gymnast than the athlete. Consequently, all high jumpers are advised to take advantage of opportunities to use a trampoline when under the guidance of a qualified instructor. The trampoline offers the luxury of extended "flight time", when the athlete can learn to adjust his body to assume certain shapes. Once learned the athlete now has new possibilities open to him, because once in the air he can twist or rotate his body to any desired shape. This being the case, it is our duty to work out the best shape of the body to take greatest advantage of this flight parabola at the high point, which should be over the bar.

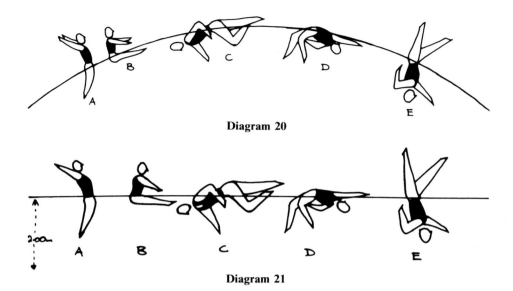

Diagram 20

Diagram 21

Here are some of the shapes possible for the athlete. See diagram 20.

C and D have most to recommend them, since the centre of gravity can be outside the body—unlike shapes A, B, E. To make the point clearer, let's have a look at this athlete at bar height. As you can see, he has in each case jumped high enough to raise his centre of gravity to a height of two metres. See diagram 21.

Provided the athlete is rotating about this long axis in C, and about the transverse axis in D, he will succeed in not displacing the bar, and therefore clear 2.00m.

Immediately the shape C is identifiable as that of the Straddle layout; while shape D is that of the Flop layout. It may be worth emphasising again that Straddle and Flop are techniques of total high jump and not just layout. The mastery of these layouts is a product of many hours of technique training,

but the number of hours spent will be very much less than those spent on approach and take-off. The following kinogram and photo sequences show the nature of the rotations which allow the athlete to negotiate the bar.

Sequence 5 Beilschmidt 11-16 on Pages 16/17

Sequence 4 Grigoreyev 12-17 on Pages 14/15

Sequence 7 Matzdorf 17-24 on Page 20

Sequence 1 Grant 11-14 on Pages 8/9

Sequence 6 Ackermann 12-16 on Pages 18/19

Sequence 2 Henkel 10-16 on Pages 10/11

Sequence 3 Simeoni 11-16 on Pages 12/13

Sequence 9 Mracnova 8-16 on Pages 38/39

Sequence 9

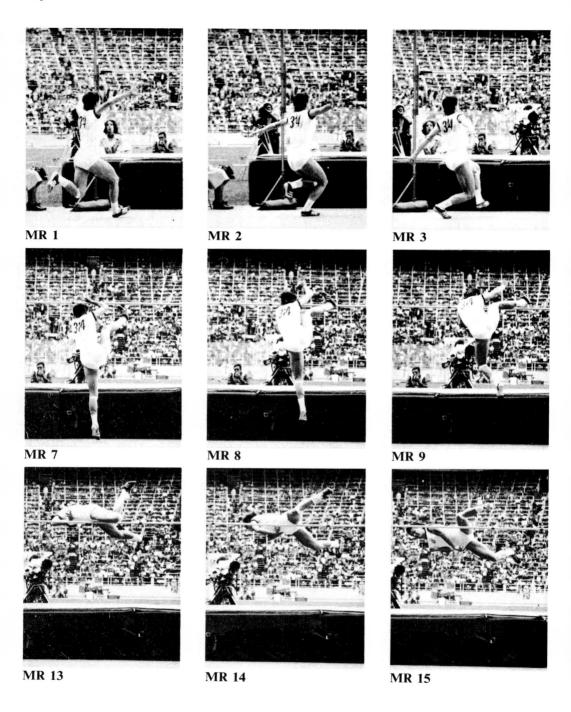

MR 1   MR 2   MR 3

MR 7   MR 8   MR 9

MR 13   MR 14   MR 15

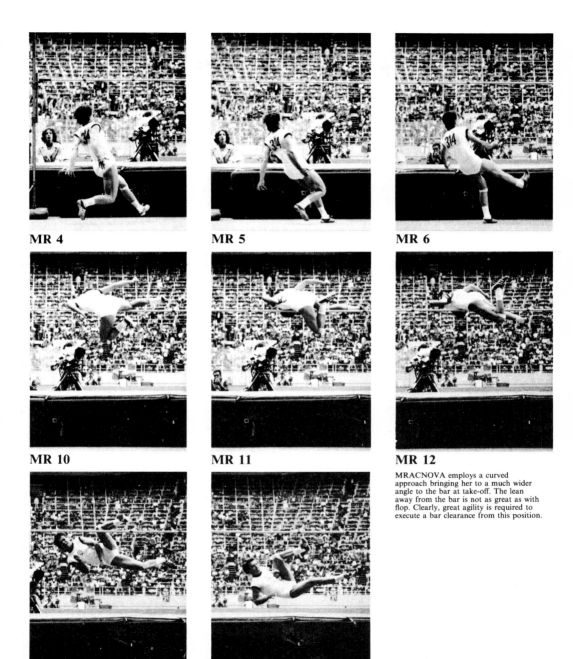

MR 4

MR 5

MR 6

MR 10

MR 11

MR 12

MRACNOVA employs a curved
approach bringing her to a much wider
angle to the bar at take-off. The lean
away from the bar is not as great as with
flop. Clearly, great agility is required to
execute a bar clearance from this position.

MR 16

MR 17

6. Developing technique of Flop and Straddle; the co-ordination of arm action; and the concept of high jump conditioning and training

This—is what—you do!

Development of technique—Flop

1. (a) Suspend a ball approximately 2 ft. (60 cm.) above the heads of the group you are coaching.
    (b) Off 3-5 strides athletes jump from one foot to try and meet the ball with their head. This should be repeated 10-20 times and used often in training at all levels. Encourage the athletes to jump straight upwards, and discourage travelling in the jump. See diagram 22.
2. Stack your cushions so that they are above head height. Off 3-5 strides athletes jump from one foot to land on their shoulders on the topmost cushion. The athletes approach the cushions from an angle of about 45° and jump from their outside foot. See diagram 23.
3. Mark the jumping area as illustrated in the diagram. Left foot jumpers start at A1, accelerate towards A2, then turn towards A3 to repeat the practice described in 2. From A2 to A3 the athletes will take three strides on a curve decided by their own strength and speed. Although the early strides may be as in normal running, these three strides are

Diagram 22

Diagram 23

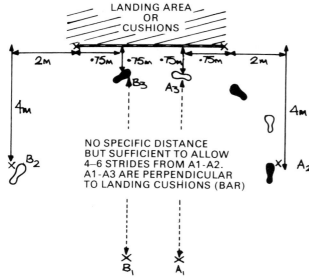

LANDING AREA
OR
CUSHIONS

2m   ·75m ·75m ·75m ·75m   2m

B₃   A₃

4m   4m

NO SPECIFIC DISTANCE
BUT SUFFICIENT TO ALLOW
4–6 STRIDES FROM A1-A2.
A1-A3 ARE PERPENDICULAR
TO LANDING CUSHIONS (BAR)

B₂   A₂

B₁   A₁

Note:
Take-off point 0.75 m. in from upright (edge of cushion) and 0.75 m. out from bar (cushion).

Diagram 24

made by placing the entire foot on the ground with each stride. Take-off is from A3. Right foot jumpers will run B1-B2-B3. Total run-up will be 7-9 strides. See diagram 24.

4. (a) Set cushions at normal height and stretch broad elastic between the uprights at hip height.
   (b) Standing with back to bar the athletes jump upwards and backwards, arching their back to land on their shoulders on the cushion. The starting position is 2 pigeon steps from cushion to heel. See diagram 25.
   (c) Gradually increase height of elastic until it reaches shoulder height. This

practice should be used every training session, where jumping technique is being worked on.

5. (a) Off one stride athletes jump from one foot to clear elastic as in 4(b) and (c).
   (b) Off three strides athletes repeat this practice whilst the following points are emphasised at take-off. (Left foot take-off).
      (i) The left shoulder is kept *square* with the left leg and *high*. It must not be twisted away or towards the bar.
      (ii) The right shoulder is turned slightly towards the left (away

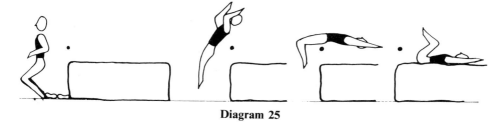

Diagram 25

41

from the bar) but is also lifted high.

Diagram 26

(iii) The right knee is kept bent for the beginner, with the foot always behind the knee.

Diagram 27

(iv) The right thigh is driven across the body towards the left hip.

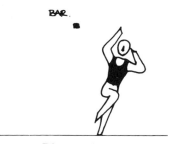

Diagram 28

(v) The hips are lifted forwards and upwards vigorously.

(vi) Both arms are punched upwards vigorously.

(vii) Once off the ground, the left heel is pulled backwards towards the head (arching the back) whilst the right leg is dropped and the heel pulled back.

Diagram 29

(viii) Once the hips are over the bar, pike thighs to chest, *then* straighten knees, finally landing on the shoulders.

Diagram 30

6. Gradually build the total jump to use the run-up as described in 3. From here the individual athlete will determine his own particular run-up curve, but by and large the last three strides should be as described in 3. Whatever happens, however, emphasise the points suggested in 5(b) at take-off and always encourage the athlete to jump *high* first, and *over* second!

7. Introduce the bar as the athlete gains confidence in his/her jumping.

Development of technique—Straddle

Assumed to be jumping from the left leg.

1. (a) Over a distance of 20-30 m, have your group of athletes running flat footed, i.e. landing heel first on every stride and taking the body weight on the

Diagram 31

whole foot, not just the toe as in normal running; do this 6-10 times. See diagram 31.

(b) Repeat running two strides with knees bent (crouch running) and jumping in the air on the third over 20-30 m. Do this 4-6 times.

2. (a) Stand athletes with weight on their jumping foot, and the other (free) leg held in front with the heel resting on the ground. Now ask the athletes to 'sit' slightly, and from this position, by vigorously lifting the free hip/ thigh, *then* straightening the jumping leg, jump in the air. Do this 8-10 times. See diagram 32.

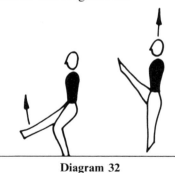

Diagram 32

(b) Repeat this exercise by stepping onto the jumping leg, then swinging the free leg. Do this 6-8 times. See diagram 33.

3. Repeat practice 1(b), using the jumping technique of 2(b).

4. (a) Suspend a ball approximately 2 ft. (60 cm.) above the heads of the group you are coaching.

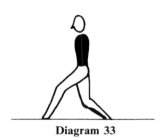

Diagram 33

(b) Off 3-5 strides athletes jump, using the jumping techniques of 2(b), to try and meet the ball with their head. Do this 10-20 times and continue to use this practice often at all levels of development.

(c) Repeat this exercise, but athletes now try to reach the free foot to the ball.

(d) Throughout these practices, the jumping leg, once it has left the ground, is turned outwards (Charlie Chaplin feet) and the knee is flexed.

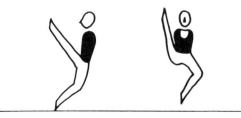

Diagram 34

5. (a) Stand group with their jumping foot along a line.

(b) The athletes jump by swinging the free leg, then turn in the air to land on the "free" foot facing in the oppo-

43

Diagram 35

site direction. The jumping action should be as in 2(b).

6. (a) Set cushions at normal height and stretch a broad elastic between the uprights at hip height.
   (b) Stand group facing the elastic as shown in the diagram. Repeat practice 5(b). Do this 6-8 times.

ARM LENGTH

Diagram 36

7. Repeat exercise 3(c), jumping over the elastic without turning in the air, i.e. it is a straight jump, emphasising the jumping action. Angle of approach and take-off point are as in the diagram. Do this 10-15 times.

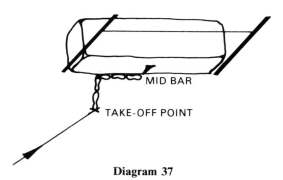

MID BAR

TAKE-OFF POINT

Diagram 37

8. (a) Slope elastic as shown.
   (b) Progress the height of the elastic at both ends as athletes now roll round the "bar" in flight. Do this until the elastic is at head height on the left. Then gradually raise the right side until the complete jump is executed. Encourage the athlete to keep the legs "bowed" throughout the flight.

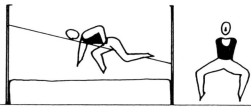

Diagram 38

Development of technique—co-ordinating the arms

1. Give each athlete in the group a skipping rope.

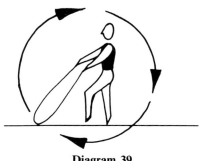

Diagram 39

(b) Instead of bringing the rope forwards and downwards towards the feet, bring it from behind so that the arms lift the rope up in front (backwards skipping). See diagram 39.
2. Without the rope athletes lift both arms vigorously as they jump from one foot to the other.
Bound from one leg to the other over 20-30 metres, lifting vigorously with the arms on each jump. See diagram 40.
3. (a) Ask athletes to spring into the air off three strides by lifting vigorously with the arms. The athletes should solve the problem of bringing both arms through on their own, but if guidance is required try the following drill. See diagram 41.

Now the athlete's technique is not quite as 'armless'.

Technique of training—Summary of Points

Rather than list a boring set of faults and corrections, attention is again drawn to the fundamentals of the event. If these are not worked for using practices relevant to each fundamental, then problems will arise—and correction is simply to go back to fundamentals:—

Approach run:

(a) *gain required velocity early* in the approach.
(b) work to *maintain speed* to take-off.
(c) *last three strides on heels or ball of foot*, depending on take-off technique.
(d) *co-ordinate arms* for take-off.
(e) *set trunk and hips* for take-off—hips rolled under.

Take-off:

(a) *free hip* drives free leg through and up.
(b) *both shoulders* lift upwards, neither must drop.
(c) *take-off hip* drives forward and upwards.
(d) *arms* vigorously lift upwards—not over.

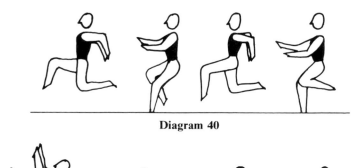

Diagram 40

Diagram 41

Clearance:

(a) watch *movement of body parts* relative to bar.

(b) *check high point* of jump relative to bar. (Most flight problems, if not traceable to approach and take-off, will be solved by frequent practice on a trampoline or with the help of a gymnast or diver).

Most high jump problems start in the approach, are then magnified in take-off and highlighted in failure at heights well below the success that should reward months of hard work. The event starts on the ground, so look to the preparation of the high jumper at this level first. The event is high jump—not a clearance technique.

The Organisation and Development of Training

A. The Growing and Developing Athlete

A training programme is specific to athlete and coach and the environment in which they work. Consequently, at best, the following should be considered as a guideline to the construction of a high jumper's training programme.

The B.A.F. booklet "Training Theory" sets out the background against which programme construction should be seen. In addition, coaches should note the following:—

Bases of Programme Construction

1. Although jumping practices may be included in their training sessions, youngsters of 10-14 years are best not to work on specific jumping schedules. Sprinting and technical basics of all events should be covered together with the gradual improvement of the oxygen transport system, and great emphasis on mobility and the ability to handle the resistance of the athlete's own body-

weight. The latter will require the thoughtful deployment of gymnastic apparatus—ropes, beams, boxes, benches, wall bars etc. Light resistances such as medicine balls can also be introduced at this level.

2. *From 14-16 years.* The schedules can now concentrate on specific work for the high jumper, with great emphasis on the increasing of strength not only in the jumping muscles, but also in the extensor muscles of the spine, those of the shoulder girdle and those which flex the spine and hip. The execution of all strength work done involving the jumping action (e.g. step-ups) *must* be done with the jumping action in mind. (Shoulders lifted, free leg swung, back straight and hips "rolled under"). All-round conditioning programmes involving the body as resistance, plus light resistances, are essential, as are sessions on and off the track for development of oxygen transport efficiency and the ability to sustain relaxed sprinting. Other events should augment the training and competitive programmes—especially hurdles, long jumps and sprints. Neither maximum nor sub-maximum loadings are recommended for squats at this stage, because the growing spine is at considerable risk of injury. Consequently, light-medium load front squat with many repetitions is preferred, but even here there must never exist the problem of loss of balance leading to spine injury. The need for considerable conditioning of the spine extensors and flexors, plus the muscles of the hip and shoulder complexes, must have top priority in these years as preparation for later heavy work on the extensors of the knee and hip.

3. *Over 16.* The role is simply progressive resistance and the ability to express great force at speed. This area of the programme should grow naturally from the

previous years of preparatory work, and sophistication of individual conditioning and technique will evolve through competitive experience and experimentation based on sound guidance. A word of caution is suggested for the mature athletes of 16 and over. There is a great risk that so much work will be done on the muscles in the front of the thigh that there is disproportionate strength existing between those muscles and those *behind* the thigh (and with this situation comes great injury risk to those muscles, the hamstrings). Consequently, jumpers are encouraged not to neglect the hamstrings in training. Exercises to strengthen them will include work for knee flexion (e.g. knee curls) and hip extension (e.g. spine hyper-extension while suspended, face inward, from wall bars).

4. Try to avoid the situation where there are maximum competitive demands repeatedly made on the athlete. One competition per week should be sufficient demand made of an athlete in the season, with the occasional two competitions/weeks.

5. Exercises are only as beneficial to the jumper as the manner in which they are performed. *Think* what relationship the exercise has to the jump—then perform the exercise with this relationship in mind. A series of exercises is not simply a load of work to be got through, but a number of practices to be perfected in the interest of competitive advantage. Here are some exercises that may offer a starting point for coach and athlete to develop their own variations:—

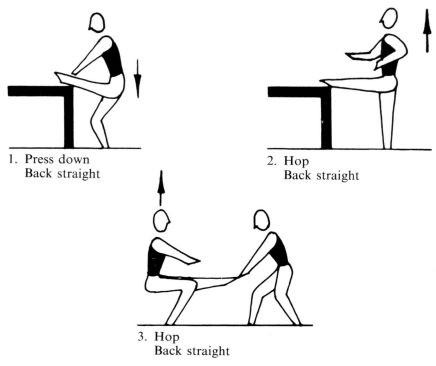

1. Press down
   Back straight

2. Hop
   Back straight

3. Hop
   Back straight

Diagram 42

47

4. Swing leg
   Step up
   Leg straight

5. Change feet
   Back straight

6. Jump   On and off boxes to finish by jumping up to a basketball ring
   and/or   Two feet together
   Hop   Two feet astride

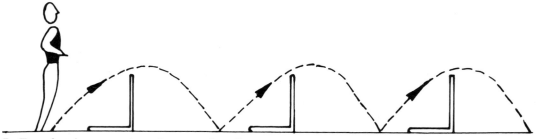

7. Two feet jumps or hopping over hurdles

Diagram 42

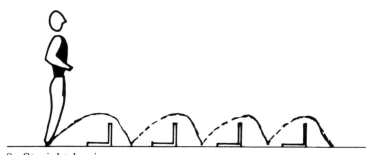

8. Straight leg jumps
   (Straight back)

9. Knee lifts with
   medicine ball

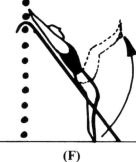

10. Pull medicine
    ball through with
    straight leg

11. Hold thigh to chest
    and straighten knee

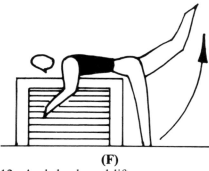

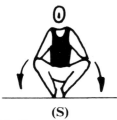

(F)
12. Arch back and lift
    heels as high as possible

(F)
13. Swing feet up to
    wall bars

(S)
14. Press knees outwards
    and downwards

Diagram 42

(S)

15. Walking over hurdles emphasising hurdle trail leg recovery with alternate legs

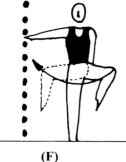

(F)

16. Pull knee across to opposite hip

(F)

17. Stretch chest up to ceiling

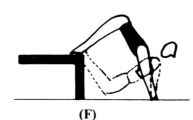

(F)

18. Alternating pike and arch

19. With medicine ball stand up with back always straight

20. With medicine ball and holding body at this angle, turn to right and left

21. With back arched, and medicine ball, turn to left and right

Diagram 42

22. Push medicine ball with straight leg from one foot to another

23. Roll ball away and then back again

(S)
24. Jump on spot by swinging free leg

25. Arch back to throw ball to receiver

26. Pull knee up across body against pulley resistance (F)

27. Standing broad jump

28. Crouch walking (90° knee) with medicine ball 20–30 m. jumping in air each third stride

29. Squat jumping with medicine ball

Diagram 42

30. Jump on spot by vigorously lifting medicine ball

Also jumps decathlon etc.

I must emphasise again that these exercises are offered only as ideas.

Heavy weights and strength

As far as heavy weights and strength are concerned, the following are again, suggestions.

1. 90° Squat

2. Heel raise

3. Leg press

4. Step ups with leg swing. Walk into the exercise

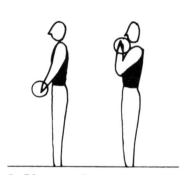

5. Biceps curl

6. Bench press

7. Forward and side alternate dumbell raise

Diagram 43

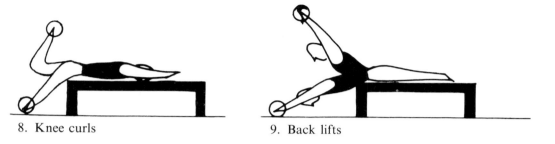

8. Knee curls   9. Back lifts

10. Curls

Diagram 43

High jumpers appear to gain advantage from using the indoor season as a second competition period in the year's programme. According to Matveyev, high jump shows a 5.05% annual improvement with "double periodisation" (indoor and outdoor seasons); and 2.4% annual improvement with "single periodisation" (outdoor season only). Diagram 44 shows the phasing of training for single and double periodised years.

The reciprocating ebb and flow of intensity (quality) versus extent (quantity) of loading might be considered as taking the pattern illustrated in Diagram 45.

The distribution of types of training in the various phases of the year are suggested as in Table 2, for the different levels and ages of athletes categorised as:—
    a. 10-14 years
    b. 15-17 years
    c. 17-18 years
    d. Novice Seniors
    e. Experienced Seniors.

I				II		III		IV	V		VI	
Nov	Dec	Jan	Feb	Mar	Apr	May	Jun	Jul	Aug	Sep	Oct	SINGLE
	I	II	III$_1$	I		II	III$_2$	IV	V		VI	DOUBLE

KEY: I — Preparation Period, Phase 1
             II — Preparation Period, Phase 2
             III — Competition Period
             IV — Recovery and Preparation Period
             V — Major Competition Period
             VI — Transition Period

Diagram 44

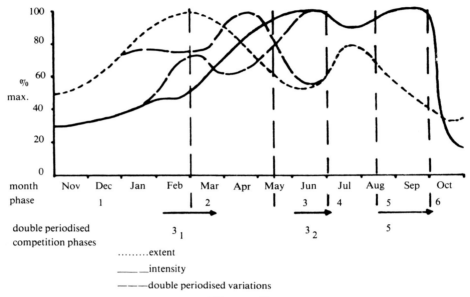

Diagram 45

Table 2

	I			II			III			IV			V			VI		
	G	S	C	G	S	C	G	S	C	G	S	C	G	S	C	G	S	C
a.	70	10	20	60	20	20	50	20	30	60	20	20	50	20	30	80	10	10
b.	60	20	20	50	25	25	50	20	30	50	25	25	50	20	30	70	20	10
c.	50	25	25	40	25	35	25	25	50	45	30	25	15	25	60	75	15	10
d.	50	25	25	40	25	35	25	25	50	45	30	25	25	25	50	75	15	10
e.	35	35	30	25	35	40	10	40	50	20	40	40	10	40	50	80	10	10

Figures represent % training units in that particular area.

KEY: G —General Training
S —Special Training
C —Competition Specific Training

General Training

This is defined as training for the development of the whole body. A basic all-round
programme is implied with, above all, the
establishment of a sound foundation of
aerobic endurance, general strength and
general mobility. Such a programme will
include:—

**Category
of
Athlete**

**Type
of
Training**

a. 1. Circuit-type work e.g.
chins   sit-ups
dips   back lifts
squat-thrusts   squats
trunk twists

2. Jumper's circuit e.g.
   standing long jump
   standing triple jump
   standing triple bound
   standing five-bounds
   standing 10-spring jumps
   2-foot zig-zag jumps
   2-foot successive jumps over
   hurdles
   straight-leg jumps
   short approach multiple hops and
   bounds
3. Fartlek over undulating country
   and including bounding uphill/
   downhill.
4. Repetition runs in sets of 3-5 over
   30 m-200 m, ranging in purpose
   from speed—speed endurance—
   strength endurance.
5. Other events—especially jumps
   and hurdles.
6. Mobility.
7. Medicine ball throwing and resistance circuits.
8. Games e.g. basketball, volleyball,
   hockey, squash.

b. 1. General weight training, e.g.:
Biceps curls	Abdominal curls
Bench press	Back lifts
Power clean	"Short hammer"
Half squat	swings
Hamstring	Heel raise
curls	
2. Jumper's circuit—as for "a" plus
   hopping/bounding on/off boxes.
3. Fartlek as for "a".
4. Repetition runs in sets of 3-6 over
   distances from 30 m-600 m, ranging in purpose from speed—speed
   endurance—strength endurance.
5. Other events—especially hurdles,
   jumps and multi-events.
6. Mobility.
7. Medicine ball and weighted jacket
   workouts.
8. Games, e.g. basketball, hockey,
   volleyball, squash.

c,d,e. 1. General weight training:—
   Biceps curls
   Leg lifts/curls
       from hyper-extension
   Bench press
   Hanging hyper-extension
   Power clean
   "Short hammer" swings
   Half squat
   Jumping slide squats
   Heel raise
   Dumbell raises
   Hamstring curls
   Leg press
2. Jumper's circuit as for "b" with/
   without weighted jacket.
3. Fartlek as for "a" with many
   changes of speed, hill sprints,
   leaping over logs, across ditches,
   on sand, in surf, etc.
4. Repetition runs as for "b".
5. Repetition runs for strength endurance, e.g.
   60 m-200 m High knee lift (Skip
   "A")
   60 m-200 m Brumel runs
   60 m-200 m Bounding
   60 m-200 m Skipping for height
   60 m-200 m Harness runs

   or for balance, e.g.
   60 m-200 m Hurdles at various
   spacings.
6. Mobility
7. Medicine ball and weighted jacket
   work-outs as for "b".
8. Games, e.g. basketball, hockey,
   volleyball, squash.

Special Training

The object here is to develop a special series
of exercises which involve the joint and
muscle dynamics of high jump. These will:

i. isolate the many components of the
   whole technique, e.g. two-arm dumbell
   lifts—imitating the arm action.

ii. combine several components of the whole technique, e.g. Brumel walk with weight on shoulders, to take-off every fourth stride—imitating the last strides to take-off.

Exercises involving the whole technique, e.g. jumping with a weighted jacket, may find their place more in the competition-specific than special exercises area of training. Throughout all these practices, the basics of the event technique are never ignored. The following are merely examples and the coach and athlete should use initiative to expand this list in light of the availability of wall bars, boxes, benches, ropes, beams, weights, weighted jackets, medicine balls, sand dunes, stadium steps, etc.

    a. Step-ups with medicine ball held at arms length—in front.
Walk-in step-up jumps with leg swing for height.
Unloaded Brumel runs with take-off every fourth stride.
Brumel runs.
Leg swing jumps or cossack jumps.
Free knee lifts against light resistance.
Hurdle mobility (straddle).
Spine hyper-extension from hip flexion (arch from pike) without weights (flop).
Etc.

b. & d. Walk-in step-up jumps with leg swing for height—with light weights on shoulders.
These may also be performed using an inclined ramp rather than a bench/box.
Free knee/leg specific movement patterns against light resistance.
Skipping with light weight on shoulders.
Brumel runs with weights jacket, taking off every fourth stride.
Hopping over low barriers (hurdles) with weights jacket.

Three-stride jumps to head ball with weights jacket.

c. and better d. Depth jumps from 0.50 m-1.10 m.
Cossack hops with weights jacket or weights on shoulders.
Curved approaches and take-off (with weights jacket) to head suspended objects.

    e. Step-down with resistance.
Rebound jumps with weights on shoulders.
Etc.

Competition-Specific

This is the technique completely rehearsed, both in parts, and more importantly, as a complete movement in the competition situation. The area varies from a shade of special training to actual competitions which eventually are presented in an increasing variety of conditions. In the total extent of training, it plays the smallest part.

It would be pointless to run through a-e in this area, because in the final analysis, all that is involved here is the learning of technique. The basic format of progression might be seen as:—

1. Demonstrate technique.
2. Athlete attempts whole technique.
3. One fundamental is emphasised.
4. Athlete attempts to establish that fundamental.
5. Athlete attempts whole technique.
6. Another fundamental is emphasised, etc.
7. Once the athlete appears to have learned the fundamentals of the technique, then work in patterns such as:—
    i. approach
    ii. take-off
    iii. approach—take-off
    iv. clearance
    v. take-off—clearance
    vi. approach—take-off—clearance

TABLE 3: Model technique analysis sheet for the Fosbury Flop (after G. Tidow).
The figure drawings A to M are referred to in the "Reference" column.

FOSBURY FLOP	PHASE	REFERENCE		CRITERION	ASSESSMENT
	I Approach: PENULTI- MATE STRIDE	A B BC B C	1 Foot plant 2 body/trunk 3 arms 4 front supp. 5 supp. knee 6 rear arm 7 arms	ball contact/curved path inclination/slight forward lean counter arm swing heel lead yielding held back parallel/behind trunk	
	II Approach: LAST STRIDE	D DF E F F EF	8 trunk 9 supp. leg 10 take-off leg 11 arms 12 body/trunk 13 foot plant 14 free leg	upright horizontal pushing action fast & active plant/pre-tension/'long' starting double swing inclination/backward lean 'through' the bar/optimal take-off pos. bending/forward-upward movement	
	III TAKE- OFF	FG FH FH GH H H H	15 take-off leg 16 arms 17 free leg 18 free knee 19 arms 20 shoulders 21 body	minimal & passive yielding active double arm swing active knee drive 'opening'/block in horizontal pos. blocked/bent lifted/horizontal vertical/parallel to upright	
	IV RISING OPENING	I I IK IK IK K K	22 head 23 outside arm 24 body 25 arms 26 free leg 27 back 28 head	view: along the bar 'leading' longitudinal axis rotation 'opening' lowering parallel to bar backward movement	
	V LAYOUT	KL L L L L L	29 arms 30 hips 31 legs 32 back 33 head 34 longit. axis	extended/'diving action' hyperextended/elevated bent/directed downwards 'arched' thrown back rectangular to bar	
	VI RECOVERY	LM M M M M	35 pelvis 36 head/trunk 37 hips 38 legs 39 arms	active lowering 're-active' countermovement active bending synchronous active knee extension bending	
	VII PREPARA- TION for LANDING		40 head 41 hips 42 arms 43 body 44 legs	raised bent/blocked spreading in 'L-position' extended/directed upwards	

Ideas for Practice on:

Approach

— tape course of curve for floppers
— keep take-off point approx. 0.75 × 0.75 m from near upright
— establish sufficient reference marks to ensure accuracy
— "Groucho Marx" walk on the last three strides—but *back must remain vertical*
— swing arms across body in approach

Take-off

— jump up to head a ball
— jump up onto cushions
— jump up to kick/knee a ball
— check foot, shoulders, hip etc. for fundamentals

Approach—take-off

— arm co-ordination now essential—start by skipping(rope) backwards—jumping on spot and circling arm as in triple, etc.
— drive for 5-7 strides, heels settle for final stride/three strides according to take-off emphasis.
— emphasise "scissor action" of take-off/ free leg passage at take-off.

Clearance

— jumping backwards over elastic.
— vaulting over gate/barrier in "frog-leap" position.
— 1-3 stride——clearance at elastic; slope elastic away from Straddle jumper.
— introduce bar *late*.

Take-off—clearance

— short approach work, etc.

Approach—take-off—clearance

— full jumps at various heights—do not go for excessive heights until patterns of movement are well established.

The idea of applying a checklist approach to technique analysis can bring valuable system and discipline to technique evaluation in training and competition. Gunther Tidow introduced this approach for use by German coaches and a modified form of his "model technique" analysis sheet for the Fosbury Flop is set out in Table 3.

On the subject of strength training, it is suggested that the coach reads and thoroughly understands the contents of the B.A.F. publication "STRENGTH TRAINING". This said the following additional points are worth noting.
1. It is now recognised that to work at the same intensity all the time will develop strength slower than if intensities are varied from unit to unit. Thus the macrocycle of one month might look as in Table 4.
2. If steep increases in jumping strength are sought, sets of jumps exercises should be alternated with orthodox weights exercises for the legs.
3. Jumps with weights must not cause too great a technical compromise.
4. In special preparation for a major competition, a 5-week macrocycle has been suggested, involving 3 weeks

Table 4

Week	Sun.	Mon.	Tues.	Wed.	Thurs.	Fri.	Sat.
1	3 × 5 × 85	—	3 × 7 × 75	—	3 × 5 × 85	—	3 × 7 × 75
2	—	3 × 3 × 90	—	3 × 6 × 80	—	3 × 3 × 85	—
3	4 × 5 × 85	—	4 × 2 × 95	—	4 × 5 × 85	—	4 × 2 × 95
4	—	4 × 3 × 90	—	4 × 7 × 75	—	4 × 3 × 90	—

Table 5

PHASE OF YEAR

CATEGORY OF ATHLETE	I	II	III	IV	V	VI
a.	1. Circuits and badminton 2. Fartlek/2 × 5 × 150m. 3. mobility, jumps circuit, other events.	1. jumps circuit and basketball. 2. 3 × 150m: 120m: 90m/ 3 × 5 × 30m. 3. competition specific, other events.	1. jumps circuit and other events. 2. 3 × 150m: 90m: 60m/ 3 × 5 × 30m blocks. 3. competition.	1. jumps circuit and basketball. 2. 3 × 150m: 120m: 90m/ 3 × 5 × 30m. 3. competition.	1. jumps circuit and other events. 2. 3 × 120m: 90m: 60m. 3. competition.	1. volleyball, etc. 2. Fartlek. 3. hockey, etc.
b.	1. general weights and squash. 2. Fartlek and mobility. 3. 6 × 200m/4 × 300m. 4. jumps circuit and special exercises.	1. general weights and basketball. 2. competition specific and special exercises. 3. 100m-200m-300m-200m-100m/3 × 150m: 120m: 90m. 4. jumps circuit and 3 × 5 × 30m blocks/ 3 × 4 × 20m-20m-20m (sprint-decelerate-sprint).	1. jumps circuit and other events. 2. competition specific, special exercises and mobility. 3. 3 × 5 × 30m blocks over hurdles/acceleration runs over 60m. 4. competition.	1. general weights and basketball. 2. competition specific and special exercises. 3. jumps circuit and 3 × 5 × 30m blocks/ 3 × 4 × 20m-20m-20m (sprint-hold-pace-sprint). 4. competition specific and special exercises.	1. jumps circuit and other events. 2. competition specific, special exercises and mobility. 3. 3 × 5 × 30m blocks over hurdles/acceleration runs 60m. 4. competition.	1. volleyball, etc. 2. swimming and sauna. 3. Fartlek. 4. hockey, etc.
c.&d.	1. general weights and handball. 2. hard Fartlek and mobility. 3. jumps circuit and special exercises. 4. 2 × 4 × 200m/5 × 300m. 5. competition specific and special exercises.	1. general weights and easy running. 2. jumps circuit and strength endurance runs over 60m-200m. 3. competition specific and special exercises. 4. 4 × 100m-150m-200m/ 2 × 4 × 150m. 5. competition specific and special exercises.	1. general weights and jumps circuit. 2. 3 × 5 × 30m blocks over hurdles/2 × 4 × clock blocks 20m-80m. 3. competition specific and special exercises. 4. 3 × 5 × 20m-20m-20m (sprint-decelerate-sprint)/ 3-4 × 120m. 5. competition.	1. general weights and easy running. 2. other events and strength endurance runs over 200m. 3. special exercises and mobility. 4. 3 × 100m: 150m: 200m/ 2 × 3 × 150m. 5. competition specific and special exercises.	1. c. competition specific and jumps circuit. d. hard Fartlek and mobility. 2. 2 × 5 × 30m blocks over hurdles/2 × 4 × clock blocks 20m-80m. 3. competition specific and special exercises. 4. 3 × 5 × 20m-20m-20m (sprint-hold-sprint)/ 3-4 × 120m. 5. competition.	1. hill walking. 2. swimming and saunas. 3. Fartlek. 4. tennis. 5. dancing.
e.	1. general weights and basketball. 2. special exercises and 2 × 5 × 150m. 3. competition specific and basketball. 4. special exercises and 2 × 4 × 200m/5 × 300m. 5. general weights and massage. 6. competition specific and other events.	1. general weights and basketball. 2. competition specific and special exercises. 3. 3 × 150m-90m-150m/ 3 × 120m-60m-120m. 4. competition specific and special exercises. 5. 3 × 5 × 20m-20m-20m (sprint-decelerate-sprint)/ 3 × 150m and special exercises. 6. competition specific and special exercises.	1. general weights and special exercises. 2. competition specific. 3. 6 × 30m, 3 × 60m, 2 × 90m and special exercises/ 4 × 30m, 3 × 40m, 2 × 60m and special exercises. 4. competition specific and special exercises. 5. 3 × 5 × 20m-20m-20m (sprint-decelerate-sprint)/ 3 × 150m and special exercises/3 × 150m and special exercises. 6. competition.	1. general weights and basketball. 2. competition specific and special exercises/ 4 × 30m. 3. 3 × 150m-90m-150m/ 3 × 120m-60m-120m. 4. general weights and mobility. 5. 6 × 200m/3 × 300m. 6. competition specific and special exercises.	1. general weights and special exercises. 2. competition specific and special exercises. 3. 6 × 30m, 3 × 60m, 2 × 90m and special exercises/ 4 × 30m, 3 × 40m, 2 × 60m and special exercises. 4. competition specific and easy running. 5. 3 × 5 × 20m-20m-20m (sprint-hold-sprint) and special exercises/3 × 150m and special exercises. 6. competition.	1. orienteering. 2. swimming and saunas. 3. golf. 4. surfing. 5. skating. 6. riding.

increase in extent, while holding intensity at 75-85% range, followed by an increase to 90-100% over the last 2 weeks, during which time, work such as that described in "2" above is used, accompanied by a drop in extent. This must, of course, be seen against a heightened intensity of special and competition specific work.

5. It should be noted that increased maximum strength has *not* been shown to produce an immediate improvement in performance in high jump. There appears to be a delay where strength increase is stabilised, before improvement shows itself. Consequently—in situations such as the 5-week special preparation macrocycle, training for strength should be seen as being closely matched by training to *apply* strength increase to jumping.

Table 5 is advanced as a suggested series of yearly training plans, based on the foregoing points. It will be seen that certain activities eventually become absorbed in others. Thus, "jumps circuit" may well be embraced by "special exercises" and so on.

These suggestions are set out in 3, 4, 5 or 6 days per week—this representing various types of microcycle. Where oblique lines occur (/), this represents alternating units from week to week.

B. Advanced to National and International Athletes

At National and International level, the athlete's programme of training should be considered as a progression based on a sound foundation of work such as that suggested in Table 5. To succeed at this level, it seems that the athlete should meet certain anthropometric requirements. Height, bodyweight, and the coefficient of height/weight serve as useful guides to the "structure" of the International high jumper. The range of the coefficient is remarkably narrow, as demonstrated by statistics of world ranked athletes in 1992 (Tables 6 and 7). It seems reasonable to take such statistics into account when assessing the suitability of athletes for progression to advanced level.

The differential of "height jumped" minus "standing height" provides an indication not only of jumping ability, but also to a certain extent, of technical efficiency. Consequently,

Table 6.

Male High Jumpers – Top 12 Barcelona Olympics 1992

Name	Height	Weight	Coefficient	Personal Best	Differential
Javier Sotomayor	1.96	82	2.39	2.44	0.48
Patrik Sjoeberg	2.00	82	2.44	2.42	0.42
Artur Partyka	1.92	69	2.78	2.37	0.45
Tim Forsyth	1.96	73	2.68	2.34	0.38
Hollis Conway	1.83	65	2.81	2.40	0.57
Ralf Sonn	1.97	85	2.32	2.39	0.42
Troy Kemp	1.87	69	2.71	2.35	0.48
Marino Drake	1.94	73	2.66	2.34	0.40
Charles Austin	1.94	73	2.52	2.40	0.56
Dragutin Topic	1.97	77	2.56	2.37	0.40
Gustav Becquer	1.84	70	2.63	2.30	0.46
Steve Smith	1.84	70	2.63	2.37	0.53
Max/Min 1976 Olympic Competitors	1.96/1.79	86/69	2.77/2.24	2.31/2.20	0.43/0.28

Table 7.

Female High Jumpers – Top 12 Barcelona Olympics 1992

Heike Henkel	1.81	64	2.83	2.07	0.26
Galina Astafei	1.81	60	3.02	2.00	0.19
Joamnet Quintero	1.88	69	2.72	1.98	0.10
Stefka Kostadinova	1.80	60	3.00	2.09	0.29
Sigrid Kirchmann	1.81	63	2.87	1.95	0.14
Silvia Costa	1.79	60	2.98	2.04	0.25
Megumi Sato	1.78	57	3.12	1.95	0.17
Alison Inverarity	1.81	60	3.02	1.96	0.15
Debbie Marti	1.71	55	3.11	1.94	0.23
Danuta Jancewicz	1.89	74	2.65	1.93	0.04
Birgit Kahler	1.82	60	3.03	1.94	0.12
Tanya Hughes	1.83	53	3.45	1.97	0.14
Max/Min 1976 Olympic Competitors	1.87/1.71	76/48	3.58/2.42	1.96/1.87	0.20/0.00

Table 8.

a. height............m   b. weight............kg   c. coefficient (height/weight)............

d. height jumped............m

e. coefficient (height jumped/height)............

f. Sargent jump............cm

g. standing 5 hops (right leg)............m

h. standing 5 hops (left leg)............m

i. coefficient (g/h)............m

j. standing 30m sprint............sec.

k. sprint endurance run 450m............sec. (from standing start)

l. maximum parallel squat............kg

when evaluating the high jumper, it seems expedient to apply several testing procedures in order to identify specific strengths and weaknesses. Table 8 sets out those test procedures which seem most appropriate for the high jumper.

NOTES ON EVALUATION

a. height: Athletes should be approx. 1.78+ (female); 1.86+ (male) at maturity.

c. Height/weight: Athletes should be in the ranges (2.7-3.1) female and (2.4-2.7) male. If less, then the athlete may need to lose weight; if more, then weight gain via strength gains (muscle hypertrophy) may be indicated.

e. height jumped/standing height: Best index of jumping efficiency. A sound technique on a good basis of conditioning should provide a differential of 10 cm + (female) and 20 cm + (male).

f. Sargent jump: A score of less than 50 cm (female) and 60 cm (male) indicates a need for general and maximum strength improvement. A score of 50 cm-55 cm (female) and 60 cm-65 cm (male) indicates a need for maximum and special strength improvement.

A score of 55 cm+ (female) and 65 cm+ (male) indicates a satisfactory foundation of jumping strength for a high jumper to build upon by increasing maximum and jumping strength with minimal weight gain.

g. and h. 5 hops right/left: Less than 12.00 (female) and 13.50 (male) indicates a need for basic and elastic strength work.

12.00-13.00 (female) or 13.50-14.75 (male) is a sound basis upon which to build basic jumping strength *and* elastic strength.

13.00 m+ (female) or 14.75 m+ (male) indicates that the athlete is ready for maximal strength, plus special exercises such as depth jumps, and box work, weights jacket work, etc.

i. coefficient—difference 5 hops right and 5 hops left: Balanced strength programme gives a difference of 80-100 cm.

j. 30 m sprint: This is an index of basic speed status. 4.3 sec. or faster for female and 3.8 sec. or faster for male, are good rules of thumb. (Time taken from first foot strike).

k. Sprint endurance run: This is an index of basic endurance status. Females should not be slower than 18.5 nor males slower than 17.5.

l. parallel half squat: The athlete should consider his target—5 repetitions with a bar equal to twice his/her own body weight and use as a power index 10 repetitions with a bar equal to his/her own bodyweight *timed*.

Preparation of International standard athletes for specific major competitions is a feature of training cycles which may span from 1 to 4 years. It is clear that such athletes employ a double periodised year most effectively. There are, however, differences in the structure of the training programme. Drechsler (Germany) suggested that there were two principal variants.

Variant 1—Successive or Accentuated Training

This type of programme is advanced on the principle of developing from general to specific fitness by phases in series. This variant is favoured by Drechsler—and is used by both Beilschmidt and Lauterbach (see diagram 46).

Variant 2—Complex Training

This type of programme is advanced on the principle of developing all areas of fitness in parallel but with different emphasis in each phase of the year. Although each phase sees a change of progression from the more general work in early winter, to the more specific work of summer, each phase, macrocycle and microcycle contains a blend of training in all relevant areas of fitness. This is more a feature of U.S.A. training systems than European (see diagram 47), but has been used to some effect with Dalton Grant (2.36m), Kim Hagger–heptathlete (1.90m), Janet Boyle (1.92m) and Barbara Simmonds (1.92m).

According to Tancic (Germany) both variants imply approximately 6 competitions in 6 weeks in the indoor season, and 12-20 competitions in 12-16 weeks in the outdoor season. Training detail is a logical application of training principles to develop

i. general athletic ability
ii. running ability
iii. jumping ability
iv. flight ability
v. a stable non-athletic environment

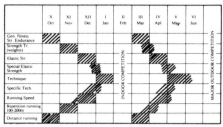

Diagram 46 (from Drechsler). Application of principal types of training over a given year.

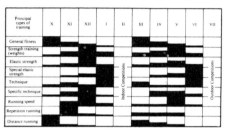

Diagram 47. Distribution of principal types of training using variant 2—complex training (based on Drechsler's terminology).

Examples of practices for such developments are as follows:—

i. *General athletic ability* (and active recovery) (general endurance, mobility, strength).
   1. 30-60 mins games, e.g. basketball, squash, football, tennis, swimming, etc.
   2. Mobility units (30-45 mins).
   3. General strength units 'A' e.g. circuit training, stage training, general activity unit, etc.
   4. Outdoor activities, e.g. skiing, climbing, cycling, etc.
   5. Mini competitions involving other disciplines, related activities, etc.
   6. Relaxation/recuperation, e.g. autogenic training, massage, sauna, etc.

ii *Running ability* (technique, speed, special endurance, general endurance)
   7. General endurance runs, e.g. Fartlek (30-40 mins), diagonals of football field (20-30), etc.

8. Special endurance runs, e.g. 2 × 4 × 60 secs with 2 mins and 5 mins recovery, 2 × 3-4 × 300 m—same recoveries, 6 × 200 m with 3 mins, 2 mins, 1 min, 3 mins, 2 mins recovery.
9. Special endurance runs (strength), e.g. 6-10 × 150 m high knees, 6-10 × 150-200 m with weights jacket and springy stride, 6-10 × 150-200 m with weights jacket and skipping etc.
10. Special endurance runs (speed), e.g. 2 × 4 × 120-150 m—85% max. with 2-10 mins recovery, 3 × (150-120-90 m) 90 secs/3 mins recovery, etc.
11. Spatial awareness runs, e.g. low hurdles at varied distances (60-200 m) (i.e. hurdle 1-2 = 7 stride spacing, 2-3 = 3 stride spacing).
12. Balance runs, e.g. 6-10 × 60-100 m accelerate-decelerate-accelerate-run flat footed etc.
13. Acceleration runs, e.g. 2-3 × 3-4 × 30 m-30 m-30 m (sprint-hold-sprint) OR (sprint-decelerate-sprint), 6-10 × 100 m as 50 m stride—50 m sprint, 6-10 × 80 m of 10 strides fast—10 strides hold—10 strides fast, etc.
14. Speed runs, e.g. 2-3 × 3-4 × 30-50 m, short clock—20-30-40-50-60-50-40-30-20 m, 2-3 × 3-4 × 40 m from blocks on straight or curve, etc.
15. Varied pace runs, e.g. 100-200-300-200-100 m at, for example, 15, 32, 51, 32, 15 pace with 1, 2, 3, and 2 mins recovery, etc.
16. Curve runs, e.g. figure 8 runs round three posts, etc.
17. Transition runs, e.g. 6 strides, acceleration—weight forward—3-5 strides maintain speed—weight on heels/flat foot—move hips, etc. into take-off etc.
18. Technique runs, e.g. 10-12 × 60-120 m emphasising various aspects of running technique—arm action, leg drive, knee lift, etc.

iii. *Jumping ability* (max. strength, elastic strength, strength endurance, technique).
  19. General strength units 'B'—orthodox lifts—cleans, various types of squat, various types of arm/shoulder press, various types of trunk/abdominal exercises.
  20. General jumping strength units, e.g. hopping, bounding, step-ups with weight alternating in sets of 5-10 with step-down rebounds without weight, running/bounding/hopping up steps, multiple horizontal and vertical jumps in sand, skipping with weight on shoulders, light resistance work for trunk and abdomen, etc.
  21. Special jump strength units, e.g. two-foot straight knee jumps over 6-8 hurdles 1 m apart—at 30-45 cm height, 3-4 stride approach jumps over 4-6 × 76-106 cm hurdles—this exercise performed 10-20 times = 40-120 jumps, free leg swings with resistance on thigh, arm action using dumbells, short approach with weights jacket to jump and head/kick a suspended ball, 3-7 strides in half crouch to take-off, etc.
  22. Technique jumps, e.g. varied stride approach (1 stride—full approach) working on points of technique—with graded height of bar. Broad areas of exercises included those aimed at the

  i. *take-off*:
     jumping action (jumping legs/hips), posture (trunk/hips alignment), momentum action (free leg and arms).

Table 9.

Distribution of types of practice according to Drechsler's "Principal Types of Training".

General Fitness and Strength Endurance (general athletic ability)

1, 2, 3, 4, 5, 6, 9, (25)—the latter to be covered from time to time throughout the year. Some coaches build in 1 hour per week to ensure that the environment remains stable.

Strength Training—Weights (jumping ability)

19—varying in structure of loading throughout the year. Mainly a gradual progression using 50%-100% varied loadings, but occasional steep progression over 5 weeks mixing with elastic strength work—prior to "peaks".

Elastic Strength (jumping ability)

20—varying in actual practices to ensure broad progression without boredom. Fatigue should not come into this work unless it is a strength endurance session early in the annual cycle.

Special Elastic Strength (jumping ability)

21—as for 20.

Technique (jumping, running, flight—ability)

22i, ii, iii, 23, 24.

Specific Technique (jumping, running, flight—ability)

22i, ii, iii, 23, 24, 11, 12, 16, 17, 18.

Running Speed (running ability)

13, 14, 18.

Repetition Running (running ability)

8, 10, 15.

Distance Running (running ability)

   ii. *approach*:
rhythm, acceleration-transition, consistency of take-off foot placement and into take-off.

   iii. *flight*:
rotation (*not* from take-off side), joint actions relative to bar, high point, length of parabola, etc.

iv. *Flight ability* (special mobility, technique).

  23. Ground practices, e.g. work at steeplechase barrier for Straddle recovery, "bridging" for Flop recovery, related mobility exercises.

  24. Flight practices, e.g. Straddle rotation sloping (away) bar/elastic, box (elevated) backward take-off over bar/elastic for Flop exercise, trampoline work, flight rotations off top of sand dunes, etc.

v. *Stable environment*

  25. Coach-athlete conferences, e.g. discuss diet, sleep, management of studies, domestic problems, motivational stimuli, etc.

Each coach, athlete and situation will demand an individual interpretation of practices. This intepretation will not only vary in terms of the practices—but also in terms of the structure of loading (intensity:extent) and in terms of the training ratio (training:recovery). Table 9, then, must be seen in this light, where areas of work are suggested as requiring to be included under the headings in variants 1 and 2.

Finally, Table 10 is included as an example of how the training detail for an 8 week macrocycle might be set out.

Developing straddle and flop

TRAINING PHASE PLAN

Phase No: ....2.....................

Name (Athlete/Team):

Commencing: ....20th. November.

Ending: ....7th January...

No. of Weeks: ....8..........

Objectives: 1. General Strength (+compensatory)
2. General endurance
3. General mobility
4. Specific strength
5. Basic technique

Programme Microcycle	Cycle of ....7.....Days		Repeated ......8......Times		
Day	Unit 1	Unit 2	Unit 3	Unit 4	Unit 5	Unit 6
1.		T1		Strength B		Blitz
2.	High Jump ②				Strength A ①	
3.		T2		Strength B		Mobility
4.	High Jump ②				Strength A ②	Circuit
5.		T3		Strength B		Mobility
6.	R	E	S	T		
7.	High Jump ①	T4			Strength A ③	
8.						
9.						
10.						
11.						
12.						

Progression by Weeks or Sessions

Unit Detail		1	2	3	4	5	6	7	8	9	10
T1 3×	120m	15.5s	→	15.0	→	14.5	→		(2min)		
	90m	11.25	→	10.8	→	10.35	→		(10min)		
	60m	7.2	→	6.9	→	6.6	→				
T2 3× 3×	Drive – Hold – Lift (30m – 30m – 30m)					(Walk) (10m)					
T3 2×3 ×150	21.75		20.25		18.75		17.5		(2 min) (10 min)		
2×4 ×100	14			13		12		11.5	(2 min) (10 min)		

Strength A

1/3 Front Squat	3× 10	3× 10	3×5 ×85%	3×7 ×75%	4×3 ×90%	3×5 ×85%	→		
1/2 Slide Squat	3× 10	Test	5×2 ×95%	4×3 ×90%	5×2 ×95%	5×2 ×95%	→		
Cleans	3× 10	Test	3×5 ×85%	3×7 ×75%	4×3 ×90%	6×1× 100%	→		
Back combin.		4×5×					→		Fwd. -Side- Back
Deltoid combin.		4×6×					→		Fwd. – Side
Hip combin.		4×6×					→		Ext.: Flex.: Abd.: Add.:

Blitz   (Max. in 60 secs)

Press-ups

1/2 squat jumps

Tuck-ups

Pull-ups

| Potato race | · · · ·   ⊢→ | 3m × | 3m × | 3m × | 3m × | 3m | (WR?) |

Med. ball side lift

Table 10.

Unit Detail	Progression by Weeks or Sessions									
	1	2	3	4	5	6	7	8	9	10
Circuit	4 ×					(non-stop)				
Pole climb	3						Against clock			
Box jumps	24									
Hanging w.scr.wipers	4									
Dips	10									
Skipping	100									
Med. ball lift	36									
Strength B										
Bounding	2–4 × 30m									
RR LL RR	2–4 × 30m									
Hop R.	2–4 × 30									
Hop L.	2–4 × 30m									
Slalom Two-foot	2–4 × 30m									
Spring jumps	2–4 × 20m									
Groucho walk	2–4 × 25m									
High knees	3–5 × 50m									
3-Box routine	4–6 × 3 (× 3 box turnabout)									
Incline jumps	2–4 × 3 (10kg weight jacket)									
Step-down jumps	2–4 × 4									
High skipping	2–4 × 30m									
Walk routine	2 × { In Out	Toe Heel }	20m								
Fast stride	6 × 60m									

Unit Detail	Progression by Weeks or Sessions									
	1	2	3	4	5	6	7	8	9	10
High jump ②										
Hurdle rebounds	2–3 × 4 × 5 hurdles – 3'3"									
Straight leg rebounds	2–3 × 4 × 8 hurdles – 30cm									
Box layouts	2–3 × 4 × (place bar high)									
RRRL	2–3 × 4 × 30m									
Hurdle jumps	2–3 × 4 × 5 hurdles – 3'3"–3'6"									
Scissors	2–3 × 4 ×									
Rolling 7-stride	2–3 × 4 ×									
High jump ①	a. 6–8 × full approach – no jump									
	b. 3–5 × 4 × full approach jumps									
T4	3 × 4 × 60m 3/4 to full speed from standing									

Table 10.

Competition Notes

1. Warm up is specific to the event for which the athlete is preparing so, in addition to jogging, striding and stretching, the high jumper must attempt to simulate take-off technique and rehearse flight positions. In addition to physical rehearsal, the athlete should concentrate on a mental rehearsal of the total technique.

2. Such preparation should be geared to the athlete's starting height. In other words, there is little point in warming up for the hour before reporting time if the starting height is 1.50 m, and he is not intending to commence jumping till 1.70 m. This situation is seen in complete perspective when fields of 20-40 athletes are involved in the competition. Instead, he should commence warm-up one hour before the anticipated time at which the competition will reach his starting height.

3. "Re-warm" up 5-6 athletes before his next jump.

4. Wet-suits are not just advisable—they are *essential*, as they ensure maintenance of raised body temperature, and keep out the rain and wind. The athlete must remember to put on his track-suit and wet-suit between rounds.

5. In bright sunshine the shelter of a golf umbrella, etc. should be sought—or, alternatively, the head and shoulders should be kept covered with a blanket, towel etc. The object here is to avoid the weakening rays of direct sunlight, and track-suits *must* be worn before the competition and between rounds.

6. It is tempting to let the mind wander in competitions, due to their long, drawn-out nature, but is is essential that this is consciously worked against. Once in the competition, the athlete should *stay in the competition* and avoid the tendency to become a spectator. The struggle is as much mental as physical.

7. Check marks etc. should be measured and marked as early as possible—and preferably before competition is due to commence.

8. Spike length, heel spikes etc. should be checked before the competition. If jumping from cinder, the athlete should request that the take-off area be brushed and rolled before each round. (N.B. The area of take-off, *not* the whole take-off pad—unless it has become very chewed up!). If jumping from an all-weather surface which may have "rubbings" of grit and rubber, he should check that the take-off area is brushed clear of these "rubbings" before the competition. If jumping from a wet and "puddled" take-off pad, request should be made that the puddles be brushed clear.

9. Landing areas must be checked for gaps!. This is really a life or death precaution for Floppers. *If there is any doubt in his mind about the safety of the area, he must not Flop!*.

10. The athlete should take full advantage of his jumping time. He should request that the bar be steadied in the wind, and wait for the wind to drop before jumping. Sometimes it is useful to make a miniature "wind-sock" adjacent to the bar/ landing area to give a guide to the force and direction of the breeze. This could be arranged via the event judges, and can be made simply by sticking a cane in the ground and tying a bandage to the top of the cane. If there is movement beyond the bar, or near him, request should be made that the movement be stilled before his "time" has started. This problem often arises with the long run-up athlete who starts on the track, and he must time his effort well!

11. He must *think* about each jump. He should concentrate his attention on knowing why jumps have gone right or wrong. When a jump does go wrong, he should concentrate on correcting the

error he has made. For instance, if the bar was knocked off on the way up, was it due to a take-off too close to the bar? If so, how will he correct this? Was it due to a "flat" jump brought about by dropping the inside shoulder? If so, how will he correct this? Etc.

12. In a long competition, a still, soft drink should be available to sip from time to time.

13. The athlete should take a change of kit with him. It is extremely uncomfortable to get soaked in a wet qualifying competition, and then have to go on to a final still soaked! Dry kit will help him to get the feel that he is in a new competition—instead of a remnant from an old competition!

14. High jump officials often have a cold and miserable task in terrible conditions. They, like the Pole Vault officials, have the longest competitions to run, so during the competition, the athlete should help with any sweeping, rolling, adjustment of landing areas or retrieving of bars—and after it is over, remember to thank them. After all, they make his competition possible!

Extract from B.A.F. Rules for Competition

FIELD EVENTS

RULE 120 GENERAL CONDITIONS

Draws, Trials and Qualifying Rounds

A draw shall be made to decide the order in which competitors shall take their trials and this order should be printed in the programme. The Judges shall have the power to alter this order. Competitors cannot hold over any of their trials to a subsequent round, except in the High Jump and Pole Vault.

If competitors are entered in both a track event and a field event or in more than one field event taking place simultaneously, the Judges may allow them to take their trials in an order different from that decided upon prior to the start of the competitions.

Competitors who unreasonably delay making a trial in a field event render themselves liable to having that trial disallowed and recorded as a fault, and for a second delay at any time during the competition to disqualification from taking any further trials, but any performances previous to the disqualification shall stand for inclusion in the final result of the competition.

It is a matter for the Referee to decide, having regard to all the circumstances, what is an unreasonable delay. The following times should not normally be exceeded:

(a) in the High Jump, Long Jump, Triple Jump, Shot, Discus, Hammer and Javelin —one and a half minutes.

(b) in the Pole Vault—two minutes, the time beginning as soon as the uprights have been adjusted to the satisfaction of the competitor.

(c) when three or fewer competitors remain in the competition the time in the High Jump should be extended from one and half minutes to three minutes and in the Pole Vault from two minutes to four minutes.

NOTE: If the time allowed elapses once the competitor has started a trial, that trial should not for that reason be disallowed.

If in the opinion of the Referee the conditions warrant it, that official shall have power to change the place of the competition in any field event. Such a change shall be made only after a round is completed.

If for any reason a competitor is hampered in a trial in a field event, the Referee shall have power to award a substitute trial.

Where in any of the field events the Organisers or the Referee consider it advantageous a qualifying round shall be held prior to the competition proper.

All competitors who reach the prescribed standard in the qualifying round or pool shall compete in the competition proper. If less than the prescribed number of competitors reach the qualifying standard then the leading athletes up to that prescribed number shall take part in the competition proper; where necessary Rules 121(7), 126(3) or 130(3) shall be used to decide the qualifiers. If a tie for the final place in the competition remains after these Rules have been applied, all those competitors so tying shall be included in the competition proper.

Once competitors have reached the qualifying standard they shall not take any more trials.

If qualifying rounds or pools are held the order for taking trials in the competition proper shall be determined by a fresh draw.

Once a competition has begun competitors are not permitted to use runways or take-off areas for practice or warm up purposes.

RULE 121 GENERAL CONDITIONS

(1) Unless such details are specified in the programme, the Judge shall decide the height at which the competition shall start, and the different heights to which the bar will be raised at the end of each round. The competitors shall be informed of the details before the competition begins.

(2) Competitors may commence jumping at any of the heights above the miminum height and may jump at their own discretion at any subsequent height. Three consecutive failures, regardless of the height at which any such failure occurs, disqualify from further participation, except in the case of a jump-off or a first place tie.

NOTE: The effect of this Rule is that competitors may forego their second and third jumps at a particular height (after failing once or twice) and still jump at a subsequent height. If competitors forego a trial at a certain height, they may not make any sub-sequent attempt at that height except in the resolution of a tie.

(3) Even after all the other competitors have failed, a competitor is entitled to continue until he or she has forfeited the right to compete further, and the best jump shall be recorded as the winning height.

(4) After the competitor has won the competition the height or heights to which the bar is raised shall be decided after the Judge or Referee in charge of the event has consulted the wishes of the competitor.

(5) All measurements shall be made perpendicularly from the ground to the upper side of the cross-bar where it is lowest. A steel or fibre-glass measure should be used. Alternatively a scientific apparatus which has a certificate of accuracy from a nationally recognised standardising organisation may be used. Any measurement of a new height shall be made before competitors attempt that height. In the case of a record claim the officials must check the measurement after the height has been cleared.

NOTE: Judges shall ensure, before commencing the competition, that the under-side and front of the cross-bar are distinguishable, and that the bar is always replaced in a similar manner.

(6) (a) The height shall be recorded to the nearest 1 cm below the height measured if that distance is not a whole centimetre.

(b) Unless there is only one competitor remaining the bar shall not be raised by less than 2 cm in the High Jump after each round.

(7) Ties

Ties shall be decided as follows:

(a) The competitor with the lowest number of jumps at the height *at which the tie occurs* shall be awarded the higher place.

70

(b) If the tie still remains, the competitor with the lowest total of failures throughout the competition up to and including the height last cleared shall be awarded the higher place.

Example: High Jump

	1.67m	1.72m	1.75m	1.77m	1.80m	1.82m	1.85m	Total Failures	Position
Jones	—	xo	o	xo	—	xxo	All	4	2=
Smith	o	o	o	x—	xo	xxo	failed	4	2=
Brown	o	o	x—	o	xxo	xxo	three	5	4
Black	o	—	—	xxo	xxo	xo	times	5	1

Jones, Smith, Brown and Black all cleared 1.82m and failed at 1.85m
0 = cleared   x = failed   — = did not jump

(c) If the tie still remains:
   (i) if it concerns first place, the competitors tying shall have one more jump at the lowest height at which any of them finally failed, and if no decision is reached the bar shall be lowered or raised 2 cm. They shall then attempt one jump at each height until one competitor clears a height and the remaining competitor(s) fail at the same height. Competitors so tying must jump on each occasion when resolving the tie.
   (ii) if it concerns any other place, the competitors shall be awarded the same place in the competition.

Example:

	1.75m	1.80m	1.83m	1.86m	1.88m	Total Failures	Jump off			Position
							1.86m	1.84m	1.86m	
Green	o	xo	xo	xxx		2	x	o	x	2
Johnson	—	xo	xo	—	xxx	2	x	o		1
Baker	—	xxo	xo	xxx		3				3

0 = cleared   x = failed   — = did not jump
NOTE: All competitors shall be credited with the best of all their jumps including those taken in a jump-off of a first place tie.

RULE 122 HIGH JUMP

(1) Rules 120 and 121 apply.

(2) The uprights or posts shall not be moved during the competition unless the Referee considers the take-off or landing area has become unsuitable. Such a change shall be made only after a round has been completed.

(3) Competitors may place marks to assist them in their run-ups and take-off, and a handkerchief, or similar object, for sighting purposes may be placed on the cross-bar.

(4) The distance of the run-up is unlimited.

(5) Competitors fail if they:
   (a) in the course of a jump dislodge the bar so that it falls from the pegs; or
   (b) take-off from both feet; or
   (c) touch the ground, including the landing area, beyond the plane of the uprights either between or outside the uprights with any part of the body, without first clearing the bar, unless in the opinion of the Judge no advantage is gained.

Bibliography

High Jumping—V. M. Dyatchkov—Track Technique   36

High Jump—D. C. V. Watts—A.A.A. booklet

Dossier: Fosbury Flop—Document I.N.S.—Athletisme   787

How to arrive at a good run-up in Flop—Siegfried Heinz—Die Leichtathletik   8 & 9/1973

Flop with elements of straddle—technique of the future?—Dr. Herbert Hopf—Die Leichtathletik   19/1972

Basic principles of coaching high jumps—Sandor Noszaly—Madrid Conference   January/1973

Fosbury did not Flop—F. W. Dick—S.A.A.J.C.C. Coaches' Convention November/1971

Physiology of Joints—Kapandji—Published by Livingston

Take-off technique—Prof. M. Osolin—Madrid Conference   January/1973

Straddle or Flop—V. M. Dyatchkov—Der Leichtathlet   40/1971

Fosbury Flop High Jump Style—B. Wagner—Madrid Conference January/1973

Combination of Flop and Straddle—a Progress?—Horst Herter—Die Leichtathletik   19/1972

Flop—for whom? Straddle—for whom?—C. Vittori—Madrid Conference January/1973

Analyzing the Fosbury Flop—K. Kerssenbrock—Athletika January/1970

Matzdorf v. Brumel—Kerssenbrock and Spilar—Track Technique January/1972

The High Jump Approach—T. Chityakov—Track Technique   June/1970

Run up and take-off in Flop—J. Jarver—Modern Athlete and Coach December/1971

Preparation for Training and Competition in High Jump—Erich Drechsler Germany—International Coaches' Convention—Edinburgh 1977

Modern High Jump Technique—Dragan Tancic—Die Lehre der Leichtathletik 23-26 (May-June) 1978.

Acknowledgements

I would like to express my deepest gratitude to professional and honorary colleagues, both in the UK and internationally, who have helped me collect and understand the materials contained in this booklet.

I would also like to thank secretarial staff for translating illegible writing into understandable text, and in particular, thank Barry Willis for his usual extraordinary editing work on this booklet.

Frank W Dick, O.B.E.
Director of Coaching, B.A.F.